Praise

"If you are single, married, or just stuck in a dead end late night texting war with the Scorpio across the hall, this book is for you. I laughed, I cried, I looked up two Exes on Facebook."

> ~Jenny Mollen-Actress, New York Times bestselling author

"This book was like a big dose of spiritual medicine. Thank you for reminding me I have a friend in the stars."

> ~Lisa Rinna of the Real Housewives of Beverly Hills

"I wish I had this book when I was single so I could have bypassed all the dbags I dated!"

> ~Nicole "Snooki" Polizzi of the Jersey Shores and Snooki & JWOWW

"This book is the perfect tool for dating. I'm going to make sure all my clients and friends get one stat. Bravo!"

> ~Patti Stanger, The Millionaire Matchmaker

By Sabra Ricci

Lobsters for Leos, Cookies for Capricorns: An Astrology Lover's Cookbook
Sexy Star Sign Cooking: An Astrology Cookbook for Lovers

By Jenny McCarthy

Belly Laughs:
The Naked Truth About Pregnancy and Childbirth
Baby Laughs:
The Naked Truth About the First Year of Mommyhood
Life Laughs:
The Naked Truth About Motherhood,
Marriage, and Moving On
Louder Than Words:
A Mother's Journey in Healing Autism
Healing and Preventing Autism:
A Complete Guide (with Dr. Jerry Kartzinel)
Mother Warriors:
A Nation of Parents Healing Autism Against All Odds
Lust, Love, & Faking It:
The Naked Truth About Sex, Lies, and True Romance
Bad Habits: Confessions of a Recovering Catholic
Jen-X: Jenny McCarthy's Open Book
Stirring the Pot:
My Recipe for Getting What You Want Out of Life

Dirty Sexy Funny

ASTROLOGY

SABRA RICCI
JENNY MCCARTHY

COOKIN PRODUCTIONS, LLC
Maui, Hawaii

Printed in the United States of America. For information, address Cookin Productions LLC, P.O. 880255, Pukalani, HI 96788

www.sabraricci.com
www.sabraricciastrology.com

www.jennymccarthy.com
www.jennymccarthysdirtysexyfunny.com

Cover and Interior Illustrations by Samray Design: Elizabeth Souza and Brian Farnham

Book Interior Design by KarrieRoss.com

LIBRARY CONGRESS CATALOGING-IN-PUBLICATION DATA

Ricci, Sabra and McCarthy, Jenny,

Dirty Sexy Funny Astrology / Sabra Ricci and Jenny McCarthy

ISBN: 978-0-9861615-0-6 Paperback
978-0-9861615-2-0 E-Book
978-0-9861615-3-7 Distributor

Dedication

To all those who
have been called weird, strange,
or odd for having a different point of view.
Never let your voice be silenced.
The truth shall set you free.

Contents

Acknowledgements ix

Foreword xi

Introduction ixx

Astrological Guidelines for Sex xxi

Chapter 1 Aries – The Adventurer 1

What Aries Is All About 3

Who Gets Them Hot And Not So Much 8

Aries Celebrities And Dirty, Sexy, Funny 15

Chapter 2 Taurus – The Organizer 21

What Taurus Is All About 23

Who Gets Them Hot And Not So Much 29

Taurus Celebrities And Dirty, Sexy, Funny 35

Chapter 3 Gemini – The Communicator 43

What Gemini Is All About 45

Who Gets Them Hot And Not So Much 50

Gemini Celebrities And Dirty, Sexy, Funny 56

Chapter 4 Cancer – The Nurturer 63
    What Cancer Is All About 65
    Who Gets Them Hot And Not So Much 70
    Cancer Celebrities And Dirty, Sexy, Funny 76

Chapter 5 Leo – The Leader 87
    What Leo Is All About 89
    Who Gets Them Hot And Not So Much 94
    Leo Celebrities And Dirty, Sexy, Funny 100

Chapter 6 Virgo – The Analyst 111
    What Virgo Is All About 113
    Who Gets Them Hot And Not So Much 118
    Virgo Celebrities And Dirty, Sexy, Funny 124

Chapter 7 Libra – The Negotiator 133
    What Libra Is All About 135
    Who Gets Them Hot And Not So Much 140
    Libra Celebrities And Dirty, Sexy, Funny 146

Chapter 8 Scorpio – The Lover 153
    What Scorpio Is All About 155
    Who Gets Them Hot And Not So Much 160
    Scorpio Celebrities And Dirty, Sexy, Funny 166

Chapter 9 Sagittarius – The Traveler 175
    What Sagittarius Is All About 177
    Who Gets Them Hot And Not So Much 182
    Sagittarius Celebrities And Dirty, Sexy, Funny . . . 188

Chapter 10 Capricorn – The Executive 197
What Capricorn Is All About. 199
Who Gets Them Hot And Not So Much 205
Capricorn Celebrities And Dirty, Sexy, Funny . . . 211

Chapter 11 Aquarius – The Intellectual 221
What Aquarius Is All About 223
Who Gets Them Hot And Not So Much 229
Aquarius Celebrities And Dirty, Sexy, Funny. . . . 236

Chapter 12 Pisces – The Crusader 247
What Pisces Is All About. 249
Who Gets Them Hot And Not So Much 254
Pisces Celebrities And Dirty, Sexy, Funny 261

Acknowledgements

First of all, I want to recognize my co-author and collaborator, without whom this book would not have the dirty, the sexy, and the funny. My special thanks to my friend for being my partner in crime on this exciting journey and for all the support throughout the years. You are truly an inspiration to all those that know you and someday, in the not too distant future, you will be deemed a hero for your brave stance for giving a voice to those that don't have one. I've said it once and I'll say it again, please don't ever change. I love you Jenny McCarthy!

Kudos to Jenny's Assistant, Jill Mele, for being the liaison and all your hard work coordinating schedules and keeping us on point to meet our deadlines. You're the best!

My heartfelt thanks goes to my longtime friend Gail Tredwell, our self-publishing consultant extraordinaire. Your extensive knowledge made this process seamless and we could not have done this without you. I would highly recommend Gail to anyone looking to self-publish.

A special shout out to Monique Brooks Cocco at Sunset Social Media Relations for all the savvy work you do behind the scenes that doesn't go unnoticed. Just want you to know how much we appreciate you.

Editor and researcher, Alexandra Pennebaker, your fine eye for detail is flawless and greatly appreciated.

Much appreciation to Samray Designs: Elizabeth Souza and Brian Farnham for the cover and interior illustrations. You brought your own unique vision to this project.

Karrie Ross, for the remarkable interior book design.

Justine Belson Photography for your spectacular photos and phenomenal eye for just the right shot.

Elizabeth Beauchamp!!! Where do I even start? For always bringing a unique and interesting perspective into my life since childhood. Astrology, health food, yoga! Those things are all pretty hip in 2015, some even mainstream, but the late 60's and early 70's put you into the hippie or just downright weird category. I am so grateful for your weird now. Thank you for always being there and ready to come along with me on my latest crazy venture. Your ongoing support, collaboration, and boundless energy (Aries-The Original Energizer Bunny). In fact, for keeping me going when I wanted to quit or at very least crash for the evening. I love you and appreciate everything you do for me. You are the hardest working woman I know.

I want to thank my literary agent, Susan Crawford, for believing in me, and, Marcia Markland, and all the other people at Thomas Dunne Books who made my first two books possible and taught me the ins and outs of publishing.

To my great teacher and friend, James (Dharman) Reed. You took everything I knew about astrology to a whole new level. John Sylverson, wherever you are, thank you for all your wisdom and in-depth esoteric knowledge. Boy, did we have some great talks.

I am so incredibly grateful, humbled and blessed for the love and support from my amazing husband and best friend, Ferenc. You make me laugh every single day, keep me balanced and make it all worthwhile.

To Jim Sher, Sher Institute of Astrology and Metaphysics and our Thursday group. You all are the highlight of my week and I am so grateful to be amongst likeminded individuals.

And finally, to all my supporters, clients, and fellow astrology lovers who allow me to do what makes me the happiest!

Foreword

"You're Nuts!"

"You're Crazy!"

"No way you actually believe in that stuff!"

I am quite proud to say that I have been on the receiving end of all three of these accusations! Well, at least when it comes to astrology and its long history. See, most people hear the word Astrology and immediately conjure up an image of a Gypsy woman sitting at her crystal ball, predicting a grand future with embellishments and riches or tragedy and loss.

Contrary to most people's knee-jerk reactions, Astrology has been a useful tool in history, dating all the way back to the second millennium BC. The celestial observations were a major component in politics, language, and social culture starting in the first Mesopotamia dynasty and eventually spreading to Ancient Greece and Rome. Astrology began as an educational practice for man to better understand himself based on the alignment of the stars in the Universe.

I have used it for both self-improvement and potential boyfriend research. The uses are truly endless. When you go on to read about your Sun sign in this book, you will probably find yourself frantically nodding your head in agreement with what Sabra is telling you, both good and bad. Take the positive and negative and apply them to your daily life. This is an opportunity to address some of the bad stuff on your own before it potentially interferes with the life and relationships you want.

As far as utilizing Astrology in my love life goes, I always wanted to know if our signs were a good match, if we were compatible both in and out of the bedroom. What turns him on? What doesn't? What type of woman is his sign most attracted to? Does he value family, kids, career, etc.? The stars up above have provided me with endless insight into these questions, and I have always been fascinated by the science of it.

Throughout the years, I have found myself in relationships with numerous signs, including Capricorns, Aries, and now the love of my life, a Leo. Being a Scorpio, I am very driven, both in my career and my bed, so it's always been important to me to have a man that can keep up in all areas of my life. After forty years of searching and a lot of trial and error, I have finally found myself blissfully happy with my beautiful ball of light, Leo.

Prior to finding my Leo life partner, I would often turn to Sabra before getting too serious with any one guy. If a date was on the horizon, I'd be busy doing my astrological research to prepare for the possibility of meeting another dud or the love of my life. Imagine the conversations we would have on date number two in order to get the proper information Sabra needed to give me a full reading on who they are. For Sabra to get a full understanding of the latest loser I was dating, I had to get her their birthday and the exact time and location of their birth. This was not an easy task as I was sitting across from them in a fluorescent-lit KFC, watching them grind the extra crispy skin off of a mangled chicken breast.

At this point, I usually didn't care enough to continue and find the detailed info Sabra needed for her readings. The guy sitting across from me, mowing through a bucket of chicken that I paid for probably wasn't my match regardless of his chart saying how great he may or may not be in the sack. But other times, my ability to pin the loser was not as sharp.

When I could pull off inconspicuously getting a birth date, time and location out of my date, Sabra would provide me with a plethora of information that usually reminded me that I had, once again, attracted the loser of my dreams. With the help of Sabra, I began noticing my pattern of attracting the wrong guy, and was able to really see what it was that I needed from my mate. So, I began putting my new intentions out into the Universe and here I am today. Married to the man of my dreams. My perfect Leo. The loving lion I had always dreamt of.

Got your eye on someone of a particular sign but feeling a little uneasy on how to approach them, what to say, or how much energy to put into this relationship?

Rest assured that Sabra has some answers for you. She's broken down each sign, piece by piece, with a little *Dirty, Sexy, Funny* in mind to cover all our love life woes and keep those libidos well fed and begging for more.

Jenny McCarthy

Introduction

February of 2014 turned out to be quite the month. It started with a trip to Super Bowl XLVIII and spending a month in New Jersey with my dear friend and client, Jenny McCarthy — I've had the pleasure of working with Jenny for over ten years now, and love her even more now than I did in our first meeting on Maui. During that fortuitous month, I went back to Boston to visit my family for the weekend, which happened to coincide with Jenny's *Dirty, Sexy, Funny* debut on EPIX.

My cousins and I rallied around the TV, preparing to get our laugh on, because as you all know, Jenny is one hell of a funny lady. That evening did not disappoint; we were soon all rolling with laughter. Jenny was crushing it, but so were all the women in the line-up. One by one, as each came on stage, I sat there wondering, "What sign is she?" They all had such unique styles and stories, so naturally I had to know what the stars had to say about them. As time went on, I got to know these women, either in person while doing Jenny's *Dirty, Sexy, Funny* radio show on XM Sirius Radio, or through social media. And that's when the light bulb went off!

For those that don't know me, I eat, breathe and sleep astrology! It is my world! There isn't a day that goes by that someone isn't texting me asking, "What the hell is going on with the planets today?" I've been a student of astrology, and have been actively applying my studies to life situations since I was a teenager, and without giving my age away, let's just say it's been over 30 years. After meeting the *Dirty, Sexy, Funny* women, I couldn't help but think about how these women's sense of humor and sexual style translate to astrology and more importantly, each sign of the zodiac. My curiosity stuck and paved the way for this book.

Sabra Ricci

Astrological Guidelines for Sex

Astrology has been around since 2,000 BC, waxing and waning throughout the centuries, and steadily on the rise since the 1960s. It has long been used as a tool for finding romantic compatibility between sun signs, a practice that's led to many books on the subject. However, it can also be used to determine your hottest hook up. Sometimes the two go hand in hand, but other times, the person you have the best sex with, isn't the person who's the best love match for the long term.

Most of you check the astrology column in the newspaper every day for a quick look at what's going on for you and your significant other. So you may have a basic idea of what to look for when it comes to compatibility, but that is one tiny piece of the puzzle. There are lots of other things to consider when looking for the love of your life, some of which will be explained later.

The charts below lay out the dates of each sign and which signs are the best long-term lovers, the best one-night stands, and the ones you should stay away from. Remember that this is all about sex and the sign that will certainly ring some bells for you!

Astrological Dates:

ARIES: March 21 - April 19

TAURUS: April 20 - May 20

GEMINI: May 21 - June 21

CANCER: June 22 - July 22

LEO: July 23 - August 22

VIRGO: August 23 - September 22

LIBRA: September 23 - October 22

SCORPIO: October 23 - November 21

SAGITTARIUS: November 22 - December 21

CAPRICORN: December 22 - January 19

AQUARIUS: January 20 - February 18

PISCES: February 19 - March 20

Partners at a Glance:

Hottest Sex:

Sign	Blazing	Scorching	Sultry	Torrid	Sizzling
ARIES	Gemini	Leo	Sagittarius	Aquarius	Pisces
TAURUS	Taurus	Cancer	Capricorn	Pisces	
GEMINI	Aries	Leo	Libra	Sagittarius	Aquarius
CANCER	Taurus	Cancer	Virgo	Scorpio	Pisces
LEO	Aries	Leo	Libra	Scorpio	Sagittarius
VIRGO	Taurus	Cancer	Virgo	Scorpio	Capricorn
LIBRA	Gemini	Leo	Sagittarius	Aquarius	
SCORPIO	Cancer	Leo	Virgo	Capricorn	Pisces
SAGITTARIUS	Aries	Gemini	Leo	Libra	Aquarius
CAPRICORN	Taurus	Virgo	Scorpio	Pisces	
AQUARIUS	Aries	Gemini	Libra	Sagittarius	Aquarius
PISCES	Aries	Cancer	Scorpio	Capricorn	

Partners at a Glance:

One Night Stand (or Two):

Sign	Quickie	Booty Call	Matinee	One Timer	Tryst
ARIES	Aries	Virgo	Libra	Capricorn	
TAURUS	Aries	Taurus	Scorpio	Aquarius	
GEMINI	Gemini	Virgo	Scorpio		
CANCER	Cancer	Leo	Capricorn		
LEO	Gemini	Cancer	Virgo	Aquarius	
VIRGO	Gemini	Aquarius			
LIBRA	Aries	Taurus	Libra		
SCORPIO	Aries	Taurus	Scorpio	Sagittarius	Aquarius
SAGITTARIUS	Scorpio	Sagittarius			
CAPRICORN	Aries	Cancer	Libra	Capricorn	
AQUARIUS	Leo	Scorpio	Pisces		
PISCES	Libra	Aquarius	Pisces	Taurus	

Partners at a Glance:

Not So Much:

Sign	Frosty	Icy	Brisk	Frigid	Crisp
ARIES	Taurus	Cancer	Scorpio *		
TAURUS	Gemini	Leo	Libra	Sagittarius	
GEMINI	Taurus	Cancer	Capricorn	Pisces	
CANCER	Aries	Gemini	Libra	Sagittarius	Aquarius
LEO	Taurus	Capricorn	Pisces		
VIRGO	Aries	Leo	Libra	Sagittarius	Pisces
LIBRA	Cancer	Virgo	Scorpio	Capricorn	Pisces
SCORPIO	Gemini	Libra			
SAGITTARIUS	Taurus	Cancer	Virgo	Capricorn	Pisces
CAPRICORN	Gemini	Leo	Sagittarius	Aquarius	
AQUARIUS	Taurus	Cancer	Virgo	Capricorn	
PISCES	Gemini	Leo	Virgo	Sagittarius	

* Aries and Scorpio is a Hot Combo, but just can't overcome their differences.

Other Factors Indicating Love Matches

Venus and Mars:

Where Venus resides in your chart and her sign can teach you much about your manner of expressing love. She is the Goddess of Love and will point towards the romantic aspects of love, but will also reveal things about pleasure. Her sign and the house she is in will give you an idea about what aspect of sex is the most pleasurable.

Mars is the God of War, but he's been known to make love and not war. That's what he's about in this context. The placement, by house and sign, in the chart will give you the big picture about your sex drive. It will also point out how to go after what you want. It's about expressing your desires and how to get them.

Venus and Mars are the Divine Lovers, so while there is much to be learned about yourself from their placement (Venus in a man's chart will tell him what type of woman will grab his interest and Mars in a woman's will let her know what to look for in a man), it is really about finding your own "divine" lover. A conjunction or other harmonious aspect between a woman's Mars and a man's Venus can be a real indicator of a magical love interest. It is even more powerful if the woman's Venus makes a good connection to the man's Mars.

Sun and Moon:

The Sun, which takes a year to move through the Zodiac one month at a time, represents your personality or ego and is easily recognized by your birthdate. It has already been mentioned that connections between the Sun signs of you and another person can tell you whether the two of you have a chance at love. It is the most common thing to look at. But the Sun cozying up to another planet in your chart can also be predictive of a spark, such as an amicable relation between the Sun and Venus or Mars.

The Moon represents your emotions and how you react to the myriad of feelings that bombard you every day. Determining your Moon depends on the exact time you were born, because it moves quickly through the Zodiac each month only lingering in the signs for about two and a half days each. As with the Sun, when the Moon meshes with Venus or Mars, a romantic association is indicated.

When the Sun and Moon join together agreeably, you have integration between your personality and your emotions. This is excellent when the woman's Moon and the man's Sun are on the same wavelength and the man's Moon matches up with the woman's Sun. Even if you only have one pair, it is still favorable.

Eros and Psyche:

Eros is an asteroid that can provide insight on some of your most steamy attractions. In terms of mythology, Eros is the God of Desire and Sexual Love. In your astrological chart, it is a point where you can find what is absolutely irresistible to you. This is the place where you can feel consumed with thoughts of sexual desire. If Eros is conjunct with one of your personal planets, Sun, Moon, Venus, or Mars, he will have a very prestigious spot in your chart, and can lead to your dream sexual companion.

Psyche is the Goddess of the Soul, and can help you connect with your own soul and determine your Soul Mate through her placement in your chart. In mythology, she originally was a beautiful human maiden, the youngest of three sisters, who was so adored that Aphrodite, Goddess of Love, became jealous and bade her son, Eros to make Psyche fall in love with the most terrible man in the kingdom.

But like many boy meets girl tales, Eros took one look, fell in love, and wanted her for himself, which of course wasn't the deal. He set her up in a spectacular castle, where she had the run of the place by day, and passed the nights as Eros' spouse and companion, with one catch. She could never look under his cloak to see his face. Which of course she eventually did, and he bolted. Realizing her lover was really Eros, she begged Aphrodite for another opportunity to be with him. After completing all that was asked of her, she was reunited with her Soul Mate and given the gift of immortality and the title of "Goddess of the Soul."

So the placement of Eros and Psyche in your chart and the chart of your proposed mate is significant. A good indicator for a strong love connection is a compatible match between the woman's Eros and the man's Psyche and vice versa, especially if the aspect is a conjunction. With these features, you may find your own Soul Mate.

All of the above factors can be a rather complicated to-do, given that you need the full computations. You will get the most information in a clear-cut, straightforward manner if you have your charts prepared by a professional astrologer and receive a reading to go along with it. There are many nuances and components that you might miss without a trained eye. Along with individual charts for you and your sweetie, you may also want to get a composite chart and a synastry chart, both of which are very comprehensive and will give you more information than you ever thought you would want to know. Trust me, in the task of finding your Soul Mate, the more information, the better!

ARIES

March 21 – April 19

The Adventurer
March 21-April 19

Aries have no problem taking charge in the bedroom, just as they do in their day-to-day lives. These babies of the zodiac are like energizer bunnies with energy to spare. They want what they want when they want it. These are the ones who can go at it like rabbits, while people are having dinner in the next room, or have a quickie in the elevator on the way to their room. They have no patience to wait for a better time. Mars, their ruler, waits for nothing.

Symbol: Ram
Ruling Planet: Mars
Body Part Ruled: Brain
House Ruled: First, the house of personality, physical appearance, how others see you
Element: Fire
Color: Red
Stone: Diamond
Key Phrase: I am
Trait: Courage
Weakness: Impatience
Quality: Cardinal

What Aries Is All About

Some people don't like who they are, not me, I actually really like who I am – A LOT!

In fact, I think I'm awesome. If there were a color to describe the inside of me, I would say red because I'm HOT! Plus, I have more energy then most people. Who needs Red Bull when you're an Aries? The great thing about me is that I'm the friend you call when you want to go out and have a great time. God forbid the party is boring; I have a real problem with that. I'm forced to use my Aries powers to bring life to the mundane. I'll be the first one to dance on a table or jump into a pool in the middle of winter just to get the party going. People can learn how to have fun just by watching me.

One of my favorite qualities is being impulsive. Some would say it's a weakness, but when you really think about it, it's not. Who wouldn't want to drop everything and go to Mardi Gras? Life is meant to be worth living and I plan on doing just that whether you want to or not.

Sometimes, ok a lot of times, people get annoyed with me because I get into their business, but someone needs to tell them they're doing it wrong, right? If they would only listen to me, their lives would be so much better. I can get upset pretty quickly, especially if some asshole on Facebook posts something so idiotic. I can't take it! How can they be so small-minded? I will defend my comments on their Facebook post until they de-friend me. I don't care. I don't have time to be friends with people like that. Especially if they are prejudiced! Forget it! Drives me nuts!

At least I'm independent. Thank god! I would much rather be the leader than the follower. I can't stand it when people try to tell me what to do. "Shut up. I got this." That's what I want to scream when people try to tell me how to do something.

Also, watch out if I don't get what I want. I might have a tantrum and stomp like a toddler, but at least I fight for things that matter to me. Life is too short to not get what I want, so just deal with it.

Sometimes, I have a hard time finishing things, but it's only because I'm so impatient and get bored so quickly. Why would I want to finish something that I lost interest in? I need excitement. I'm useless unless my wick is lit.

The good news for my romantic partners is that I'm incredibly exciting in the bedroom. I can go for a long time, so I hope you get enough rest. You'll need it. And a tip for you, if you bore me in the bedroom, I might look elsewhere to get off. I want someone who is my equal in sexual drive and spontaneity, both in the bedroom and out. Aries is the primal Zodiac sign, so I revel in animalistic, arousing, and adrenaline rushing experiences. So if you walk away with bite marks after sex, at least you can say I warned you.

ARIES WOMAN:

Complicated and impulsive, the Aries isn't shy about anything. She will jump in with both feet, take charge, and fully dominate the situation. This also goes for anything sexual. She can charm the pants right off you, and if you take too long, she'll throw you down on the bed and pull them off both legs at a time. Remember about Aries wanting what they want when they want it, well it's about both sexes, but it should have been written about the woman. She won't take no for an answer when she wants sex, because she wants it now, *right now!* If you're not ready, willing, and able when she is, she can easily move on to someone who is, or you'll be doing a lot of groveling at the very least.

She is often misunderstood because she can be temperamental with mood swings, which you'll have to learn to handle if you want to get sublime sex from this hot chick. She can also be domineering, opinionated, and may go so far as to suggest, make that insist, that you accept her opinions as your own. Sounds like this woman could make you her bitch, but it will be well worth it. Any aggression she has will quickly manifest in the bedroom in ways that bring you to your knees. She has a kink factor so enjoys dirty talk, both hearing it and whispering it in your ear.

The Aries woman will be romantic and playful if you have her heart. She likes flaunting her natural beauty, but if you want her to be more dramatic, all it takes is a little flattery. Subtlety isn't her strong suit, so you'll know sooner than later if a banging is in your future. Whether she loves you or not, you can expect her to be wild in the sack, and you'll both enjoy it. You could have the reminders to prove it, a little bite mark here, a little scratch there, but don't worry they won't leave scars. And it's bound to be memorable!

ARIES MAN:

The Aries male is just as sexual as his female counterpart and even more aggressive. He's the one who'll sidle up to you at the bar, and before you know it, you've left the building with him. This goes along with his fantasy, to meet someone for the first time and be fucking before the night is over. He likes hot fast sex, and is probably the original caveman, the one who throws his woman over his shoulder and carts her back to his cave to ravish her.

He can be a bit jealous, because when he has set his sights on you, he has to have all of you, none of this "I'll see" or "Maybe." Like the Aries woman, he wants you when he wants you. Playing the tease or playing coy doesn't work on him; he'll be out the door and on to someone who doesn't play games. He's a man of his word and expects you to be the same. If you send him a text promising a wild night, you'd better be prepared to follow your words up with actions. Fool him once, maybe, but you won't get a second chance. He's apt to tear your clothes off as soon as you walk through the door just in case you had thoughts of making him wait again. This isn't as brutal as it sounds. If you left those sex messages, you wanted to do those things anyway.

The Aries man is impassioned and unorthodox, and one you're likely not to forget anytime soon. He's also enthusiastic and energetic, and wants immediate fulfillment. But these are just a few of the things that add to his charm and the tactics to get you out of your clothes and into his bed. He's a fanatic and an eager beaver. Aries is the sign of the explorer and the adventurer. He'll make an adventure out of exploring the best way to get off. But don't worry; he takes you along for the wild ride as long as you're able, willing, and wet!

EROGENOUS ZONE:

The head! This sounds suggestive, but we're talking the big head, the one that sits on their shoulders with all those big brains. So nibbling on earlobes, a flickering tongue or hot breath in the ear, fingers running through the hair, and even a little face licking (no slobbering please) are some of the things that will get an Aries ready. No long slow foreplay for them!

SEX POSITION:

Sitting in a chair facing each other! Fetishes include morning sex with a bit of wrestling and hair tugging, so they can think about it all day.

SEX PROPS:

Handcuffs! What else?

Who Gets Them Hot And Not So Much

Hottest Sex: Gemini, Leo, Sagittarius, Aquarius, Pisces

One Night Stand (or Two): Aries, Virgo, Libra, Capricorn

Not So Much: Taurus, Cancer, Scorpio (with a caveat for Scorpio)

Aries with Aries

The sex is going to be really great with these two, the first time around that is, which can be anywhere, anytime. They won't be able to control the urges to jump each other and get it on; bathroom stalls, stairwells, outdoors, it doesn't matter! This fiery combo screws and then thinks about the consequences. Besides, the adventure and risk are half the fun. And since they're quick as bunnies, there's not much chance of them getting caught, anyway. As soon as they've had a few hot sexy sessions, the battle for control begins. Neither can always be the boss nor the one on top! A love match could be possible between these two, but remember we're talking about two impatient people, who each want to be number one! So it's hot sex, then time to move on.

Aries with Taurus

Aries rushes headlong into relationships, or that should be dalliances, while Taurus takes it slow and methodical. Talk about the Hare and the Tortoise! These two have an attraction for each other that will get them to the bedroom. Yes, bedroom. That's where Taurus has all their creature comforts, down pillows, feather bed, silky sheets, candles, and all those things that get them in the mood. But Aries is going to go in there and throw all the pillows on the floor, rip off their clothes, and be on top before Taurus can get the candles lit. This can be exciting for Taurus at first, but will soon grow tiresome. Aries will be bored and that will be that.

Aries with Gemini

This can be a match made in heaven, as they can connect instantly through brilliant conversation and electric energy. Aries is a blast of energy and Gemini's ruling planet, Mercury, rules all things electric, so they will be zapping each other with static jolts of immediate attraction! Both are driven by action, so Gemini can keep up with Aries and keep them turned on. Dirty words roll off the Gemini tongue into the sensitive Aries ear, with just the right amount of flicking. And you can be sure Aries will reciprocate! The only thing that can go wrong is if they allow things to get ho-hum or boring, which most likely won't happen for these two high energy machines.

Aries with Cancer

Aries and Cancer can get off to a bumpy start, if at all. However, they do have an intuition-based sexual connection, plus Cancer has an oral fixation and can use that tongue in ways to drive Aries mad. Aries can strip that shell right off the Crab and have him or her sighing in a flash. But then brash Aries will say something to hurt the feelings of ultra-sensitive Cancer, or show up late for that home-cooked dinner Cancer slaved over, tempers flare, Cancer gets moody, and Aries is out the door leaving the good sex behind.

Aries with Leo

These two are an explosion waiting to happen, and happen it will! There's a spontaneous combustion into beautiful brilliant fireworks for both of them. That's what gets and keeps them going. As soon as they meet, it's game on! There'd better be some place close by for them to get down and dirty or there's a chance they could embarrass themselves scrambling out of the bushes butt-ass naked when the sprinkler goes on. Of course, Leo likes putting on a show and everything's a contest to Aries, so they could be the two most likely to just stop, dry off, and leisurely get dressed. As long as they can take turns being numero uno, they can go the distance.

Aries with Virgo

If there are matches made in heaven, this could be the one that was made in hell. There's just too much to overcome. Sure they are both intense, which could make for really good sex, but that's not what typically happens. They're both intelligent, can carry on good conversations, and that's pretty much where it ends. Virgo likes to plan their exploits from beginning to the ending crescendo, all the time staring deeply into Aries eyes. Or at least trying to, Aries can't be bothered. The Ram has to have spontaneity and fast hard movement, and is finished before Virgo can get into it. There lies the crux of the problem: frustration and no satisfaction.

Aries with Libra

Opposites attract, which is exactly what happens between Fire and Air, as they fan the flames of passion so to speak. Their rulers, Mars and Venus, are the quintessential Divine Lovers. But Aries is all about "me", while Libra has to make it about "we." So the battles begin. They may not be the earthly divine couple, but there will be hot sex for as long as they decide to be buddies. Then it will be on to more suitable long-term lovers for both of them.

Aries with Scorpio

This is a pairing that is hot, hotter than most can stand. Fire and water create steam, steamy hot positions unimaginable for the faint of heart. When Aries wants to be held down, Scorpio says, "I'll get the ropes." Scorpio wants to do it in the hot tub, Aries says, "At which hotel?" Nothing is off-limits for these two. It's a contest of who can be the most outrageous, over-the-top, and downright kinky. In the end, the mind-blowing sex can't be the only thing going for them; if it could, these two would be stellar marriage material. Aries is too outgoing and friendly, while Scorpio is jealous and jumps to conclusions. Aries screams and yells, while Scorpio pouts and holds on to little things to throw back later. And, and, and… you get the picture. It's the end of the greatest sexual match in history!

Aries with Sagittarius

These two Fire signs can burn the place down like a heat seeking missile. They keep things hot with humor and adventure. Neither takes things in life too seriously, but that doesn't mean they aren't responsible, just that laughter makes everything better, especially in the bedroom, on a barge floating down the Nile, on the back of an elephant in India, scuba diving a coral reef, or in any exotic place in the world. Both like the freedom to explore on their own, but will come back together as long as Sagittarius' wandering eye doesn't get them in trouble. But when you have all the hottest, dirty sex at home, why would you roam too far away? Truly a match made between the sheets!

Aries with Capricorn

Rams and Goats, while you can find both these beasts cohabitating the same field, do these two species ever meet up in rutting season? You betcha! Aries and

Capricorn are two different beings, but get them hot and they'll be humping just like their animal counterparts and just as lusty. They both take leadership roles in the bedroom as well as the boardroom, which can keep things interesting. But Aries likes visibility and public displays of affection, while Capricorn wants to keep things private. If they could just be patient with each other, they could have a chance for something other than sex, but we all know about Aries and patience. They have none!

Aries with Aquarius

This is another fire and air combo, with what looks like a more subtle connection than Aries/Gemini, but it just isn't so. Aquarius loves talking just as much as Gemini and can stimulate the Aries' big brain intellectually as well as creatively. And we're talking creative positions here. Aquarius brings a whole bag of tricks to the bedroom. They're full of guile, and know how to tease Aries into thinking the end is close right before backing off a few times to drive Aries crazy. Then Aquarius takes full control, and together they have an experience like a dam bursting. No one else can get away with this, but Aquarius can teach Aries that some things in life *are* worth waiting for.

Aries with Pisces

At first glance you may think that the gung-ho Aries and the dreamy Pisces don't have a chance of any interaction let alone getting in the sack. But this just isn't so. These two can make a spiritual connection, think tantric yoga, because Aries loves any adventure and Pisces is just the one to lead the way. Pisces doesn't mind being ordered around; they love to serve and service. So these two can have a bit of heaven on earth, or a good dreamy spiritual encounter.

Aries Celebrities And Dirty, Sexy, Funny

Robert Downey Jr.:

Howard Stern got right to the point on the *You Tube Howard Stern Interview*[1] when he asked Robert Downey Jr. about his rep of compulsive pleasuring himself, to the point of him being a serial spanker. Robert said that was all before he was twelve. True to his style Howard asked about Robert's sex life with his producer wife, Susan; how many times a week, etc.? Robert confessed that when they have down time, or are on vacation, it's 2 or 3 times a week. Other times, they'll go bat shit crazy if they don't have sex right now. He told *People*[2] that the secret to their happy marriage involves lots of showers, loofahs, and knowing when they both need a little "me" time.

Aries can be self-involved and very into taking care of their own needs first. That is until The Ram settles down, then it's all about being hot for the one they love, and that's just what Robert is doing.

Steven Tyler:

Steven Tyler told *Elle*[3] that he had his first sexual experience at the tender age of seven with a pair of twins. Wonder if they were Geminis? He also shared with *SPIN*[4] that he and a band mate shared many a night in intimate encounters. One particular night, they shared a bed with two girls. What a surprise the next morning when the guys woke up to find they had a "Blue Plate Special" of seafood. Crabs all around! Time to get out those tiny combs!

Impulsive may be the motto for Aries, but then they have to live with the results. Steven probably thought this sounded like a good idea at the time, if he thought about it at all. The Aries man also lusts after adventure, so maybe the guys should have gone crabbing where they could have caught the real thing!

Lady Gaga:

Lady Gaga talked to the *Daily Mail*[5] about her sex life. She definitely has the persona of the hot Aries down, complete with the meat dress. Aries women have been known to treat men like pieces of meat, love 'em and leave 'em, if you can't keep up with me you're outta here. You would think that the scantily clad, over-the-top vixen would have been having hot sex all the time, but that isn't the case. She told Howard Stern[6] that she's in a monogamous relationship with her love, Taylor Kinney. Howard asked her if she'd consider a threesome, bringing another woman into the bedroom. She'd only say that it sounded like fun.

Aries is very independent, but when they find the right person, they're ready to settle down. So everyone should get it loud and clear that Gaga isn't messing around!

Kristen Stewart:

In an interview with *Vogue*[7], Kristen Stewart raved about her boyfriend and how much she loved him. She even went so far as to say she thought she wanted to have his babies. Then she told the surprised interviewer that she loved the way he smelled, and he also loved her smell. He was into licking her armpits. But whom was she talking about? Robert Pattinson? Or the director of Snow White and the Huntsman, Rupert Sanders?

Aries can rush into things just because they want what they want when they want it, without thinking about the outcome. Kristen, in typical Aries fashion, may have done exactly that.

Aries Celebrity List

March 21:
Scott Eastwood
Gary Oldman
Kevin Federline
Timothy Dalton
Matthew Broderick

March 22:
Reese Witherspoon
Penny Thornton
William Shatner
Lena Olin

March 23:
Judith Godrèche
Keri Russell
Chaka Khan
Princess Eugenie of York
Catherine Keener

March 24:
Jessica Chastain
Alyson Hannigan
Rosie O'Donnell
Peyton Manning
Tommy Hilfiger

March 25:
Elton John

Sarah Jessica Parker
Marcia Cross
Aretha Franklin
Katherine McPhee

March 26:
Keira Knightley
Steven Tyler
Diana Ross
Kenny Chesney
Roch Volsine
Jennifer Grey
James Caan
Amy Smart

March 27:
Quentin Tarantino
Mariah Carey
Jessie J
Nathan Fillion
Fergie
Pauley Perrette

March 28:
Lady Gaga
Vince Vaughn
Julia Stiles
Reba McEntire

March 29:
Lucy Lawless
Christopher Lambert
Elle MacPherson

March 30:
Celine Dion
Norah Jones
Eric Clapton
Warren Beatty

March 31:
Ewan McGregor
Christopher Walken
Al Gore

April 1:
Randy Orton
Susan Boyle
Ali MacGraw

April 2:
Michael Fassbender
Linda Hunt
Roselyn Sanchez
Christopher Meloni
Leon Russell

April 3:
Eddie Murphy
Alec Baldwin
Amanda Bynes

Leona Lewis
Jennie Garth

April 4:
Robert Downey Jr.
Jamie Lynn Spears
David Blaine

April 5:
Pharrell Williams
Krista Allen

April 6:
Paul Rudd
Akon
Rick Levine

April 7:
Russell Crowe
Jackie Chan
Frances Ford Coppola

April 8:
Robin Wright
Patricia Arquette
Julian Lennon

April 9:
Kristen Stewart
Jenna Jameson
Hugh Hefner
Jesse McCartney

Leighton Meester
Dennis Quaid
Cynthia Nixon

April 10:
Charles Hunnam
Steven Seagal
Mandy Moore
Omar Sharif
Michael Pitt
Chyler Leigh

April 11:
Alessandra Ambrosio
Joss Stone
Jennifer Esposito

April 12:
Shannon Doherty
David Letterman
Andy Garcua

April 13:
Ron Perlman

April 14:
Sarah Michelle Gellar
Adrien Brody
Julie Christie
Robert Carlyle

April 15:
Emma Watson
Samantha Fox
Emma Thompson
Seth Rogen

April 16:
Pope Benedict XVI
Olivia Del Rio
Martin Lawrence

April 17:
Victoria Beckham
Jennifer Garner
Sean Bean
Rooney Mara

April 18:
Kourtney Kardashian
Conan O'Brien
Zazie
David Tennant
Melissa Joan Hart

April 19:
James Franco
Hayden Christensen
Kate Hudson
Ashley Judd
Paloma Picasso
Tim Curry

TAURUS

April 20 – May 20

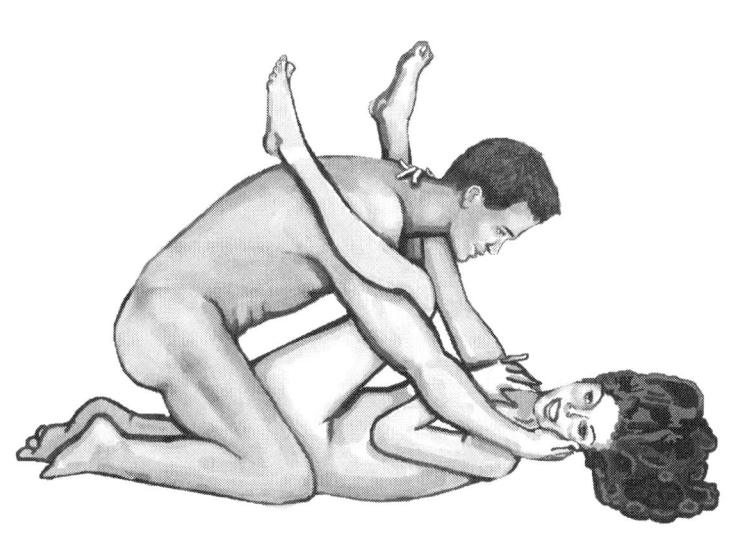

The Organizer

April 20-May 20

Taurus needs all the touchy feely stuff that comes with seduction. They like the sensual aspects of getting to the dirty deed, the wining and dining. They are big foreplay people, and love the touching that goes with it, a caress to the cheek, hands touching across the table, brushing up against each other. Silky sheets and soft fluffy pillows are a big turn on. Once this is done, the Bull will be unleashed.

Symbol: Bull
Ruling Planet: Venus
Body Part Ruled: Thyroid
House Ruled: Second, the house of your own resources and values
Element: Earth
Color: Green
Stone: Emerald
Key Phrase: I have
Trait: Dependability
Weakness: Stubbornness
Quality: Fixed

What Taurus Is All About

Slow down! I'm not in any rush to get there. I like to take things nice and slow with lots of attention to the details. Besides, in order to get things done right, we have to make sure our "I's" are dotted and our "T's" crossed.

Personally, I don't know how things would ever get done without us. We have to finish most things that Aries people begin because they are completely incapable of finishing anything. I don't mind. I like completing things. It gives me a sense of accomplishment. Just don't rush me. It's very important I do things at my speed. I've heard people call me lazy because I do things at my pace. I'll get to it when I get to it.

Fortunately, I do my job well because I like having money to spend on things that I love. I'm not reckless, but I do like to spoil myself on the finer things in life. Why should rich people be the only ones who get to enjoy a high thread sheet count? Fabric softness is very important to me. I don't know why. I would rather have one really soft cashmere sweater than eight scratchy ones.

Most would agree that I'm a really good friend to have around. Listening is my specialty, which is why I have a lot of friends. They don't know that there are only a few of them that I would consider close friends, but they don't need to know. I'm loyal and will be there to help my family and friends no matter what.

I don't really ever lose my shit, but I do get aggravated when plans change. Some say I'm stubborn, but I can't help it when someone changes their plans on me. Stick to the plan!

Some people are naïve enough to think that they can change my opinion about something. No way. I won't get into a fight about it, but its pointless to even try. When I have my mind made up, that's it. End of story.

I do make a great lover. I love long-term relationships and am very loyal. I just need to find someone that likes to stay home a lot like I do. There is nowhere more cozy and comfy than my home. I can be shy when it comes to sex, but am uninhibited when my things surround me. There's no better place than home to let me really be myself and let my hair down.

Don't expect me to talk dirty or swing from the chandelier when you take me over the edge. I am passionate and have lots of endurance, but I like to do things my way. I can go for days and never leave the bedroom. You will be so satisfied; you'll never want to look for another lover. Never. Ever. But in the case that you do, just know that I never forget and rarely let go of things. So if you just can't help yourself, you sure as hell better make sure I don't find out about it! Not only will I never look at you in the same way, but I'll also make you pay for it one way or another. Consider yourself warned!

TAURUS WOMAN:

Sex isn't a game for the Taurus woman; she's one hot cookie in the bedroom, but doesn't take any bullshit. She's very vulnerable, but you won't see it unless you have her trust. In fact, anyone she doesn't trust implicitly will find Taurus to be the Ice Queen. Of course this is a persona she takes on for protection. She's excellent at hiding her emotions, so she may be in love, but won't admit it until she's ready to put her vulnerability out there.

Taurus loves sex and is great at it. She can turn lovemaking into an art, that's how adept she is when it comes to making someone happy. Her kisses have been known to bring on the sensation without ever touching the nether regions. Ruled by Venus, the Love Goddess, Taurus has seduction down pat and will use all five senses to let you know she wants you. It's all that light-as-a-feather touching, caressing, and tantalizing that will have her lover quivering immediately. And when she's in the mood, this can go on for hours or days, bringing fulfillment over and over until you are putty in her hands.

She loves her silky sheets, soft candlelight, and romantic music anytime, but especially for setting the mood for hot sex. Role-playing is a good way to introduce her to new positions, as missionary is her old standby. But don't think that if you can talk her into an ménage à trois, that this will become an option. She will just be experimenting, making a mental note that you're not the one for her. Sure, she might enjoy it, but her jealous streak doesn't like sharing her lover with anyone, ever! So it will be your loss, and she will use her seductive ways to easily find someone else.

TAURUS MAN:

The Taurus Man is stubborn, probably the most stubborn of the zodiac. So when he sets his sights on his next lover, nothing will deter him. But as much as he is stubborn and pouts like a little boy, there is nothing he loves more than to make up. Like the female Taurus, he loves things to be slow and easy. He can make sex go on for hours and hours, waiting to make his lover happy over and over before finally falling asleep. And sleep he will! Taurus men love sleeping as much as they do making love. They need sleep to recharge their batteries so they can do it again the next day, because just like their female counterparts, they are *always* ready.

This is one passionate guy, who wants a woman by his side who is willing to stay home, share sumptuous food, and make passionate love. That doesn't mean he's a cheapskate, in fact, he loves 5-Star dining and ambiance, but values his hard-earned money, and would rather get it for bargain prices. He feels he can have the same setting at home: the soft lighting, the delectable food, the perfect music, and the comfort of his own bed. He has everything he needs to successfully seduce his lover using all five senses, without ever having to step a foot outside! Of course he isn't just limited to the bed, no, he makes good use of all surfaces in his home, including the couch and carpet.

This man is slow to get angry, but watch out if he gets to that point. She lights the spark, she'd better expect an eruption; but like I said before, he loves making up. So his lover may get the ride of a lifetime, when he's making amends. Watch out, this could become addicting if it's too good! Taurus neither wants nor needs to be told what his lover needs in the bedroom. She may make suggestions, but this obstinate and determined man is always two steps ahead. His sensual nature will already have it figured out with missionary at the top of the agenda, but he's willing to go all night, all the next day, or however long it takes to make his woman happy!

EROGENOUS ZONE:

The neck. Taurus will melt at having the neck nibbled and kissed. A flickering tongue running from right under the earlobe down to the little indentation between the collarbones will have a Taurus ready in nothing flat. You can expect to find a hickey, or several, hiding behind a turtleneck or long hair on any respectable Taurus.

SEX POSITION:

The good old missionary with a twist is the one for Taurus! Boring? Not to the practical minded Bull, especially with her legs on his shoulders! They always go for comfort first! Taurean fetishes involve anything sensual. Give them a glass of bubbly, a little chocolate, some French kisses, and they'll be all a tingle!

SEX PROPS:

Bzzzzz! Ah, the sound of an erotic battery operated massager!

Who Gets Them Hot And Not So Much

Hottest Sex: Cancer, Virgo, Capricorn, Pisces

One Night Stand (or Two): Aries, Taurus, Scorpio, Aquarius

Not So Much: Gemini, Leo, Libra, Sagittarius

Taurus with Aries

Taurus likes to take things slow; including bedroom romps, while Aries is all gung-ho about everything they do. But there's just something about Aries and all that energy that can really get Taurus going. Super-lusty Aries can get Taurus to go places they wouldn't ordinarily go. A quickie in the bathroom stall? Up against the wall in the stairwell? Oh, yeah! Things will be hot and stimulating for Taurus for as long as they want it to be, but just as quick as those gotta-hurry-up-before-we-get-caught interludes, this fling will be over, remaining as a hot memory.

Taurus with Taurus

Taurus and Taurus. What's the word I'm looking for? Boring! When it comes to Taurus on Taurus action, that's what it is, boring. I know missionary is a favorite position, which could inspire a good one-night stand, or maybe two, if they're lucky. But you can't put these two in that flat monotonous, unexciting situation over and over expecting them to feel completed every time. They'll die of boredom without some good action! So these two are better left as friends who share their thoughts on what they like, rather than trying to give it to each other.

Taurus with Gemini

This can be a fun coupling if the two can get somewhat on the same page. Taurus would rather just do it, while Gemini loves talking about it almost as much, if not more, than the actual act. The problem is Gemini can just ramble on about anything instead of talking dirty into Taurus' ear, which is never going to hold the Bull's attention. Once Taurus is bored, it's all over. If Gemini will just decide to put his or her mouth on that throat, Taurus might be up for some nice action. But who wants nice? Better pass on this!

Taurus with Cancer

Both Taurus and Cancer are into sensuous slow move-ments building to crescendos, so it may seem to get off to a *really* slow start. They need to explore each other's erogenous zones before getting on with it. But once these two are comfortable with each other, there's no stopping them. Cancer can be a bit shy about saying what they want you to do, but no worries, because Taurus will haul Cancer off to the bedroom with nary a word to ring that bell. Taurus will be the one to take care of nurturing Cancer, who's really great at taking care of others, but not so much at taking care of themselves. Both parties will never have to leave the bed, and the results will be mind-blowing!

Taurus with Leo

Leo thinks that he or she is the superstar of the bedroom and expects to be treated with adoration and accolades for the performance. Taurus doesn't buy into all the hype and thinks it's just so much bullshit. There is a chance that after throwing down a few too many drinks at some social function that they will lock eyes across the room and run off to the cloakroom, bathroom, broom closet, or maybe even a hotel room for something unexpected. In their stupor, they may think the sex was great, but sadly, in the harsh light of day, it will be a *big* disappointment.

Taurus with Virgo

Both Taurus and Virgo are so very down to earth, literally, that spontaneity won't be either's strong suit. But you can shut out the opinionated world, so who's there to judge you? Virgo may seem a bit of a prude as a partner for the ever-ready Taurus, but not to worry, Taurus has enough moxie to drag Virgo out of any shyness. Besides, Virgo *really* wants to take the big plunge and can easily be coaxed. Both are slow to get down to the actual act, but can spend hours, make that days, exploring each other's hot zones. The great thing about this match is that once they find their groove, they'll never want to stop. This one's a keeper.

Taurus with Libra

Ok, you'd think this was a match made in the Heavens. The Love Goddess, Venus, rules both Taurus and Libra, so they should be naturals at following her lead to make a love connection, or at the very least a good bang session, right? Not so much! Taurus is more serious in the approach, while Libra likes it more light-hearted and easy. Will the sex be good, and can they stay together? Yep! But probably for only half-a-minute. In the end, the Goddess just isn't enough to keep them together for the long term. But they should enjoy that one great time and store it away in their memory banks.

Taurus with Scorpio

Man oh man! Bring out the fire extinguisher! Hot, hot, hot! Taurus and Scorpio are both highly sensual and sexual; they can become addicted to each other. As long as they stay in the bedroom, on the couch, the kitchen counter, or wherever else they decide to do it. But they can only stay locked together for so long without coming up for air. And that's when the problems start. Taurus will look at Scorpio with different eyes and think, "What an ass!" While Scorpio will think that the slow and steady

Taurus is a pain in the ass! Both are unbelievably competitive and even more stubborn! So unless they plan on staying locked at the hip, these two should pass, and just relive the memories when they're feeling lonely.

Taurus with Sagittarius

Taurus can be totally turned on to the uninhibited side of Sagittarius' bedroom tactics, which make for a super-hot one-night roll in the hay. But Sag is known for his or her wandering eye, and is always looking for the next person to bed. And that's a huge sex stopper for Taurus. Jealousy and possessiveness will rear their ugly heads, and Taurus will yank the leash on Sagittarius in the blink of an eye, which will only make the Sag seek out the closest partner within range. If they ever thought there was a chance of a long-term relationship, they'd be hardly surprised once they're signing the divorce papers.

Taurus with Capricorn

Taurus with Capricorn is similar to Taurus with Virgo, all being Earth signs. Capricorn likes to take it slow and easy too. The Goat will intently go over Taurus' body with all the diligence given to a corporate contract, and when he or she finally makes the merger, it will be like all the stock options just paid off. Not only is this a match made in the bedroom, it's also one made in the money market. These two will be cashing their dividends both sexually and financially for years to come.

Taurus with Aquarius

What to say about Taurus and Aquarius? Taurus wants to get it on, while Aquarius wants to talk about it. But not in the same way fellow Air sign Gemini talks about it. Gem can at least follow through to ring Taurus' chimes. Aquarius talks about sex in heady hypotheticals, rather than in terms that will make Taurus the least bit hot. Well, Taurus will still be ready, but it'll have nothing to do with what Aquarius says; they'll be getting ready all alone in their bedroom. So there's no reason to waste time on this airy-fairy! Just go to bed and remember better matches! Aquarius won't even realize Taurus has left the room.

Taurus with Pisces

You take Earth and add Water, what do you usually get? Mud. But not with Taurus and Pisces! These two can create beautiful sculptures together. Ok, that might not sound all that exciting when you're thinking the bedroom, but just know that when these two come together, something beautiful emerges, not just some piece of crap that will dry up and crumble to dust. There may not be the usual crescendos, but Pisces' imagination and over-the-top sexual fantasies will bring Taurus to new heights; and Bull's staying power will keep the Fish content.

Taurus Celebrities And Dirty, Sexy, Funny

Megan Fox:

Megan Fox has often related how much she enjoys sex. She once told *Eonline*[8] that her libido is very high, like that of a 15-year old boy. Megan also said she'd rather stay at home having sex with husband, Brian Austin Green, than going out. Now that could really become habit forming!

There's nothing a Taurus likes more than reveling in the comfort of their own surroundings, especially when it comes to where they want to have sex. Seems like Megan is a real homebody and true Taurus.

Jamie Dornan:

Jamie Dornan can't be accused of not doing enough to prepare for his role as the infamous Christian Grey in *50 Shades of Grey*. He told the *Daily Mail*[9] that in researching what it is to be a Dominant, he went to Vancouver's Rascal's Club, a real sex dungeon, to see exactly what goes on behind closed doors. Jamie also plays the sexually driven murderer, Paul Spector, on the BBC drama, *The Fall*; so he's been well versed in dark fantasies involving sex. He also revealed that what he saw at Rascal's Club opened his eyes to a whole other dimension of sex, bondage, dominants, and submissions.

Taurus is into sensuousness and there is something sensuous about taking total charge of someone's sexual experience and submitting them to loads of pleasure. Jamie as Christian Grey provides the ultimate, role that a Taurus could wish for.

George Clooney:

George Clooney talked about his exploits in *Rolling Stone*[10]. He said he lost his virginity when he was 16, but that wasn't the first time he actually had the big O, which came much, much earlier. Apparently, when he was 6 or 7, he was climbing a rope and suddenly had his first orgasm. There must have been some serious friction against that rope! When he got to the top, he didn't know what had happened, but he couldn't believe how great it felt.

Taurus can be very self-indulgent, and it sounds like George was off to a good start from a young age. You can only imagine what he's like now as an adult!

Chris Brown:

Chris Brown got a really early start to his sex life. I mean *really* early. He reported to the *UK Guardian*[11] that he lost his virginity at the age of 8. The seductress in question was 14 or 15 years old. Talk about a baby Cougar getting it on with a cub!

Not one to take the lead, Taurus is an excellent follower. Sounds like Chris was playing a good game of "follow the leader" back in the day!

Taurus Celebrity List

April 20:
Carmen Electra
Jessica Lange
Shemar Moore
Ryan O'Neal
Crispin Glover

April 21:
Elizabeth II
Robert Smith
James McAvoy
Iggy Pop
Nicolas Bedos
Andie Macdowell

April 22:
Jack Nicholson
Nicole Garcia
Amber Heard
Jeffrey Dean Morgan

April 23:
John Cena
Michael Moore
Melina Kanakaredes
George Lopez

April 24:
Kelly Clarkson
Barbra Streisand
Véronique Sanson
Shirley MacLaine
Jean-Paul Gaultier

April 25:
Al Pacino
Renée Zellweger
Karine Ferri
Jason Lee

April 26:
Channing Tatum
Tom Welling
Jet Li
Jordana Brewster
Carol Burnett

April 27:
Nigel Barker

April 28:
Jessica Alba
Penélope Cruz
Jay Leno
Ann-Margret

April 29:
Uma Thurman
Michelle Pfeiffer
Daniel Day-Lewis
Jerry Seinfeld
Andre Agassi
Anggun

April 30:
Kristen Dunst
Lars von Trier
Stephen Harper
Willie Nelson
Dianna Argon

May 1:
Ajith Kumar
Joanna Lumley
Catherine Frot
Jamie Dornan
Tim McGraw
Anushka Sharma
Julie Benz

May 2:
David Beckham
Lorie
Dwayne Johnson
Lily Allen
Donatella Versace

May 3:
Christina Hendricks

May 4:
Kimora Lee Simmons
Pia Zadora
Lance Bass

May 5:
Chris Brown
Adele
Harry Cavill
Virginie Efira

May 6:
George Clooney
Tony Blair
Anne Parillaud
Roma Downey

May 7:
April Wilkner
Traci Lords

May 8:
Enrique Iglesias
Melissa Gilbert
Darren Hayes
Jennifer Walcott

May 9:
Dave Gahan
Rosario Dawson
Billy Joel
Jenny Mollen
Candice Bergen

May 10:
Bono
Linda Evangelista
Odette Yustman
Bob Sinclar
Wayne Dyer

May 11:
Renaud
Benoît Magimel
Linda Gibb

May 12:
Emilio Estevez
Gabriel Byrne
Emily Vancamp
Steve Winwood
Stephan Baldwin

May 13:
Robert Pattinson
Stevie Wonder
Harvey Keitel
Dennis Rodman

Stephen Colbert
Lena Dunham

May 14:
Mark Zuckerberg
Patrick Bruel
Cate Blanchett
Tim Roth
Miranda Cosgrove
George Lucas
Sophia Coppola
Robert Zemeckis

May 15:
Mireille Darc
Madhuri Dixit
Tammy Pescatelli
Andy Murray
Brian Eno

May 16:
Megan Fox
Laura Pausini
Pierce Brosnan
Janet Jackson
Tori Spelling
David Boreanaz

May 17:
Trent Reznor
Craig Ferguson

Enya
Princess Máxima of the
  Netherlands
Nikki Reed
Sasha Alexander

May 18:
Yannick Noah
Tina Fey
Sandra Cretu
Jack Johnson
Chow Yun-Fat

May 19:
Grace Jones
Drew Fuller
Sam Smith

May 20:
Cher
Samuele Papi
Joe Cocker
Timothy Oylphant

GEMINI

May 21 – June 21

The Communicator

May 21-June 21

The Gemini intellect comes to play in matters of the bedroom. They are sexually curious and well informed about erotica. Straight missionary positions don't do it for them. They love talking, so talking dirty is high on their list. Someone less verbal may be shocked by the seductive words and demands coming from a Gemini!

Symbol: The Twins
Ruling Planet: Mercury
Body Part Ruled: Lungs
House Ruled: Third, the house of communication
Element: Air
Color: Yellow
Stone: Agate
Key Phrase: I think
Trait: Responsiveness
Weakness: Scattered energy
Quality: Mutable

What Gemini Is All About

Witty and imaginative! That fits me to a tee. I can keep people entertained for hours with my witty banter, because talking is my thing, to anyone, about anything. If there's a lull in the conversation and no one knows what to talk about next, I can just make something up on the spot, and we're off and running again.

I'm a paradox. One minute, I'm as graceful as Grace Kelly at her peak, and the next, I'm down in the trenches talking dirty with the best of them. Some think these changes are mood swings, but they're just part of my dual personality. My symbol is The Twins after all! Okay, I can feel the skepticism, you're thinking split personality or a whole mess of "crazy", but you have to know me to really get it.

It's hard to pin me down or make me follow the rules. I'm very independent and do what I want to. I have to have my freedom and be free to express myself; it's critical for my mental health and stability. I won't be controlled, or let anyone be my dictator. A free spirit, that's what I am.

But I love having my friends around me. It's exciting to have me as your friend. I always keep things interesting and leave my imprint on every person I meet. I may disappear on some flight of fancy, seeing the world, and making new friends, but I'll come back with so many new stories to tell. You'll just be excited to have me back at home!

Any time you need guidance or direction, I'm your go-to person — as long as you don't get all emotional on me. I can't take it, it's too depressing. It gets me down in the dumps, which is not a good place for an airy Gemini to be. But I get right back on my feet and am ready to tell you all the latest gossip, if you're up for it. You should be, because anytime you're thinking about someone else, it means you don't have to be thinking too hard about yourself.

Everything has to be fast paced around me; too much monotony and I get so bored. That's why I have to change things up and keep it interesting. I'm putting my romantic interests on notice. If you want to keep me around, you gotta have some new moves and keep it fresh. And you can't be the jealous type. I confess to having a wandering eye, but I really, really try to not act on it when I'm in a relationship. I'd love to say a committed relationship, but that's a tough one for me.

What I really like is talking dirty while having sex. So if you're into that, you could be a keeper, the one to keep me on my toes and keep my wandering eye from going past the bedroom. But if you aren't a match for me at the sexy talk, I'll just have to find someone who is. So sad, but true!

GEMINI WOMAN:

The Gemini woman is changeable and can take on any persona; that's why she loves role-playing when it comes to her bedroom antics. She gets to be whoever she wants to be, and can act out any scenario while seducing her lover. The French maid, the pig-tailed schoolgirl, the Swedish masseuse, and the whip-carrying dominatrix are just a few of the roles she has up her sleeve. And she will definitely play each role out to the best of her ability, thrilling, tantalizing, and, eventually, leaving her conquest weak-kneed and exhausted.

This is no prim and proper woman who wouldn't say shit if her mouth was full of it. Oh no, not her. She has a mouth that would make a truck driver blush. In fact, talking dirty is her favorite form of foreplay. Don't expect to just walk up to her, grab her, and throw her down. She'll easily rebuff your efforts, and you'll be left with some uncomfortable body parts. While she is always ready to go at it, it has to be on her terms, and talking dirty is the first step. Don't be afraid to whisper some raunchy words in her ear; she'll love it. In fact, the dirtier the better because it will get her going that much faster. And once she's ready, she'll take you around the world and back again!

She is a woman who is the life of any party she attends, which makes her all the more desirable. Intellectually, Gemini is above par and loves showing it off through her witty bantering. She loves talking, but is also willing to listen and help solve issues going on in your life. But once that's done, don't go there again. She found a solution for that one, and as far as she's concerned, you need be done with it and move on to something else. If not, it will interfere with her sexual appetite, and she'll find someone who can get over their issues as fast as she can. After all, she's the woman who has more sex than any other in the zodiac, with Scorpio as a close second.

GEMINI MAN:

The Gemini man is like his female counterpart in that he's ready to go in an instant, but you have to follow his rules. No reaching under the sheets to grab him! Like the Gemini woman, he needs to be turned on through his intellect and ears. So break out the dirty-word dictionary and start talking. Grabbing him may not work, but telling him what you're going to do with him and how you're going to do it will be just what he likes. He also responds to anything that sparks his imagination, so painting a dirty, or filthy, scenario with words is the perfect way to get his mind off and running.

Another way to mentally stimulate him is through pictures showing him something he can learn, like in the *Kama Sutra* or *The Joy of Sex*. Of course, with his brilliant mind, there's always the possibility that he's already well versed on both texts. If that's the case, simply whisper, "Kama Sutra me" in his ear and he will take you through the whole book from start to finish. When he's done, you're going to be very tired. But beware, if he finds out you're tired the next day, he'll be sure to take you through it all over again. His lover won't go limp on his watch.

New positions and routines keep him from getting bored, especially when he can treat sex sessions like science experiments where he can study the effect of every little move. No dim lighting for him; he wants bright lights and mirrors to help him see all the angles. But that doesn't mean the bedroom will stay like that for long. He's just as changeable as the fem Gem, and will always be finding some new way to stimulate and appease his sexual appetites. And it will be a lucky girl who gets to go on this never-ending journey with him!

EROGENOUS ZONE:

The arm, from the top of the shoulder to the tips of the fingers, and anywhere in between. Start at the palm and fingers of the hand. Alternate between soft kisses and light circular caresses with your fingertips. Then work your way up the inner arm until you reach the armpit! Your Gemini lover will be quivering with anticipation!

SEX POSITION:

Gemini likes variety and to mix it up. A fave is the semi-seated, knees up facing each other, leaning back on those hands and elbows! Gemini's biggest fetishes are sex at super-sonic speed and quick-witted bantering.

SEX PROPS:

Gemini needs mental stimulation, so the *Kama Sutra* is perfect for kinky thoughts and new positions.

Who Gets Them Hot And Not So Much

Hottest Sex: Aries, Leo, Libra, Sagittarius, Aquarius

One Night Stand (or Two): Gemini, Virgo, Scorpio

Not So Much: Taurus, Cancer, Capricorn, Pisces

Gemini with Aries

Gemini and Aries are so hot together, they're sizzling. Better call the fire department, or better yet, the local marriage officiant, because these two can be for keeps. Gemini is a big talker who also delivers, which sets off the Aries call to action. Aries always wants to be in charge, but will allow Gemini to take charge over him or her from time to time. Neither is afraid to speak their mind, and any ensuing spats can get ugly. But finding their way to the bedroom is a surefire way to put smiles back on their faces!

Gemini with Taurus

When the chop-chop nature of Gemini is combined with the slow pace of Taurus, it sets them on a collision course in the bedroom, culminating in what seems like heaven on earth. Big shockwaves take them soaring to the highest peaks. But that's only the first time! The second time won't be so thrilling, and if, by chance, you have a third go round, it's going to feel like hell on earth. If these two had any type of friendly relationship before doing the mattress mambo, it will be almost impossible to resurrect it. Better to just be friends, because nothing else is ever going to happen!

Gemini with Gemini

Two Geminis can carry on brilliant, funny, nonsensical conversations until the cows come home, but who wants to be in a room with a bunch of cows! Sure, they'll have fun telling outrageous tales and making each other laugh, but in the end it will all just be a lot of hot air instead of hot sex. Those waggling tongues won't be good for anything else, even if they stopped moving once in a while!

Gemini with Cancer

This may be a match made in Hell! Gemini can easily manipulate the security-loving Cancer into just about anything, from role-playing as the naughty nurse, to talking so dirty it'd make even the naughtiest deviant blush. But while Gemini is busy trying to get what he or she wants, Cancer is just trying to make a real romantic commitment. This combo can leave Cancer feeling hurt and embarrassed, while Gemini flits on to someone else. Better to let this one be.

Gemini with Leo

Gemini and Leo is a great pairing. Or should I say threesome? The Lion with the Twins could be interpreted as a type of ménage à trois, which can actually be quite enjoyable. Leo usually wants control, but is willing to share calling the shots with both sides of Gemini. Both are great in the sack, both love to talk, and even when things get tense, Gemini can smooth talk to boost Leo's ego and bring them back together. These two can definitely go the distance and keep it interesting, especially since what one can't think of, the other two will!

Gemini with Virgo

You've heard the saying run, don't walk away from a situation, well this *is* a situation! Just a glance between Gemini and Virgo should be enough to head them off in different directions. This is one incompatible combo that seems odd since they both share Mercury as a ruler. But unfortunately, that's where any and all kinship ends. If they try to stick it out, they will both be sorry.

Gemini with Libra

Air signs, Gemini and Libra, are both on the same frequency. Libra is playful and Gemini loves playing roles.

Libra is receptive and the perfect recipient for Gemini's bawdy and erotic pillow talks. From the moment these two lay eyes on each other, it will be an instant love connection. The only downer is that they both love, love, love spending money, which isn't good for either's bank account. But, all they need to do is find the best money manager possible, so their spending will just consist of the amount of time they spend in bed!

Gemini with Scorpio

When Gemini and Scorpio join together for a love fest, minds will be blown. Scorpio's a master at playing love games and Gemini's game for anything. So get it while the getting is good! 'Cause after the first go round, which is hotter than hell, the house and bed may be burned to a crisp. All those flames can cause serious damage. The party-loving Gemini will invade Scorpio's privacy, and it will be over before the ashes can be swept away. Ah, but they'll always have those hot stories for later on!

Gemini with Sagittarius

They say opposites attract, and that holds true for Gemini and Sagittarius, but how long it lasts is another story. Both love to talk, so they have that in common, but that's about it. They can have fun doing the hippity dippity once, maybe twice, if they don't leave the bed in between. But once they do, they begin to get on each other's nerves faster than they can walk into the next room, so it's best for them to keep on walking.

Gemini with Capricorn

What do you get when you match Gemini, who just can't stop talking, with Capricorn, the boardroom exec type? Nothing good! Even if it's a Gemini "girl" looking for a Daddy figure, or a Gemini "boy" looking for his Mama, it's just not going to work. What you get is something that feels just south of incestuous even though there's no blood ties involved. Besides, while Gemini wants to play sex games, Capricorn would rather play a real-life game of Monopoly, buying up the Boardwalk, Park Place, and amassing a real fortune! It's a definite no on these two finding connubial bliss or bliss of any other kind!

Gemini with Aquarius

Gemini and Aquarius meet singing *Halleluiah*, because they will think they died and went to Heaven. But don't think that this just means something mundane and typical. These two wild and crazies will drag out the whips, chains, cuffs, scarves, feather ticklers, and any other kinky toy you can imagine. Gemini will pull out all the stops and Aquarius is right there with them. Plus, this combo can even make it for the long haul. Hear those wedding bells?

Gemini with Pisces

Gemini and Pisces will have more drama than any daytime soap opera. At first, there will be come-hither stares, flirting, the sexual dance, and killer sex. It'll start out so passionate, but the more they get to know each other, the more they start wondering what the hell they're doing. Gemini wants freedom, while Pisces wants someone faithful. The perfect combination, this does not make. This one falls in the no-go, hit-the-door, and don't-look-back zone.

Gemini Celebrities And Dirty, Sexy, Funny

Zoe Saldana:

In an interview with *Marie Claire*[12], Zoe Saldana laid it all out about her fave sex positions. She said she likes missionary, being on her knees, being on top, doggy-style, or standing up. Sound like there aren't many positions she doesn't like! She was also very candid on the SiriusXM show, *Sway In The Morning*[13]; about the naughtiest places she's had sex. She admitted to being a member of the Mile High Club, and to a sexy liaison on the train between New York City and Coney Island.

Geminis are adaptable and imaginative, and it seems that Zoe can adapt to any sexual situation. Plus, she is capable of thinking up all kinds of new things to keep from being bored!

Russell Brand:

During a stand-up comic routine at London's Soho Theatre in July 2013, Russell Brand told the crowd that after his 2011 divorce from Katy Perry, he thought about becoming a monk. He said that monks take a vow of chastity and never have sex with anyone. He went on to say that being married isn't that much different, since you can only have sex with one person for the rest of your life, and you end up thinking of anyone else, other than your spouse, during sex anyway.[14]

Russell may talk a good game about being a monk, and may have believed what he was saying, as Geminis have many sides. So while it would be possible for him to take a vow of chastity, it most likely wouldn't last, because talking about sex is one of Gemini's favorite things, which always leads to the real deal. To be successful, he'd also have to take a vow of silence! And we know that's never happening!

Andy Cohen:

During an interview with *Beverly Hills Real Housewife,* Lisa Vanderpump, on *Watch What Happens Live*[15], Lisa got the chance to ask Andy about his sex life, no holds barred! When she asked him about the last time he had sex with a woman, Andy replied with an emphatic "never", and that he was a Gold-Star gay. He did admit to "fooling" around with some women, but had never done the deed with any. When asked why he hadn't ever given women a real chance, he said he just liked men too much. He did, however, think being in a threesome with another man and woman could be interesting.

Every Gemini has a streak of curiosity, so the fact that Andy might consider a threesome could result in a very satisfying or memorable experience.

Angelina Jolie:

In an interview on *60 Minutes*[16], Angelina Jolie opened up about her days as a wild child admitting that she's lucky to be alive with everything she did in her early years. She also said that she's still a bad girl, and still has that sexy, dark side, but it's now only reserved for Brad. Some of her past escapades include wearing the vial of Billy Bob's blood around her neck, lip-locking with her brother, James, at the Academy Awards in 2000, and sharing about her bisexuality, especially her relationship with Jenny Shimizu. In *People Magazine*[17] she said that had she not been married to first husband, Jonny Lee Miller, she would most likely have married Jenny. But that's all water under the bridge, since that sexy side now belongs to Brad.

Geminis like variety and will get bored if they don't have it. Angelina had her share of variety before hooking up with Brad. Now, he clearly mixes it up enough to keep her wild side satisfied!

Gemini Celebrity List

May 21:
Brianna Banks
Lisa Edelstein
Mr. T

May 22:
Naomi Campbell
Novak Djokovic
CariDee English
Morrissey
Katie Price
Ginnifer Goodwin

May 23:
Joan Collins
Jewel
Kelly Monaco

May 24:
Bob Dylan
Laura Sainclair
Priscilla Presley
Kristin Scott Thomas
Patti Labelle

May 25:
Cillian Murphy
Lauryn Hill
Molly Sims

Anne Heche
Mike Myers
Ian McKellen

May 26:
Lenny Kravitz
Helena Bonham Carter
Stevie Nicks
Scott Disick

May 27:
Lisa Lopez
Jamie Oliver
Joseph Fiennes
Christopher Lee
Paul Bettany

May 28:
Kylie Minogue
Romain Duris
Monica Keena
Colbie Caillat
Carey Mulligan
Elizabeth Hasselbeck

May 29:
Melanie Brown
La Toya Jackson
Annette Bening

Adrian Paul
Rupert Everett
Melissa Etheridge

May 30:
Idina Menzel
CeeLo Green
Mark Sheppard
Wynonna Judd

May 31:
Clint Eastwood
Colin Farrell
Brooke Shields
Patti Stanger
John Bonham
Lea Thompson

June 1:
Heidi Klum
Alanis Morissette
Morgan Freeman
Alan Wilder
Ron Wood

June 2:
Wentworth Miller
Justine Henin
Nikki Cox
Zachary Quinto
Justin Long

June 3:
Anderson Cooper
James Purefoy
Jill Biden

June 4:
Angelina Jolie
Bar Refaell
Russell Brand
Noah Wyle
Michelle Phillips

June 5:
Mark Wahlberg
Pete Wentz
Kenny G
Brian McKnight
Nick Kroll
Suze Orman

June 6:
Steve Vai
Bjorn Borg
Sandra Bernhard
Paul Giamatti
Frida Gustavsson
Max Casella

June 7:
Prince
Liam Neeson

Anna Kournikova
Iggy Azalea
Tom Jones
Dave Navarro

June 8:
Kanye West
Joan Rivers
Andrea Casiraghi
Nancy Sinatra
Bonnie Tyler
Julianna Margulies

June 9:
Johnny Depp
Natalie Portman
Matthew Bellamy
Michael J. Fox

June 10:
Elizabeth Hurley
Kate Upton
Leelee Sobleski
Gina Gershon
Theresa Caputo
John Edwards
Jeanne Tripplehorn

June 11:
Hugh Laurie
Shia Labeouf

Joshua Jackson
Gene Wilder
Peter Dinklage

June 12:
Adriana Lima
George H. W. Bush
Kendra Wilkinson
Jenilee Harrison
Eamonn Walker

June 13:
Lynne Koplitz
Mary-Kate Olsen
Ashley Olsen
Chris Evans
Kat Dennings
Malcolm McDowell
Tim Allen

June 14:
Yasmine Bleeth
Donald Trump
Steffi Graf
Boy George
Lucy Hale
Marla Gibbs

June 15:
Johnny Hallyday
Courteney Cox

Helen Hunt
Ice Cube
Neil Patrick Harris
Leah Remini

June 16:
Emmanuel Moire
Alexander Astier
Eddie Cibrian
Tishara Cousino

June 17:
Venus Williams
Newt Gingrich
Kendrick Lamar
Sadie Robertson
Paulina Rubio
Greg Kinnear
Tory Burch

June 18:
Paul McCartnery
Isabella Rossellini
Ingrid Rossellini
Richard Gasquet
Julie Depardieu
Blake Shelton
Macklemore

June 19:
Zoe Saldana
Paula Abdul
Salman Rushdie
Nâdiya
Kathleen Turner
Aung San Suu Kyi
Poppy Montgomery

June 20:
Nicole Kidman
Natasha Marley
Brian Wilson
John Goodman
Josh Lucas

June 21:
Françoise Sagan
Juliette Lewis
Lionel Richie
Edward Snowden

CANCER

June 22 – July 22

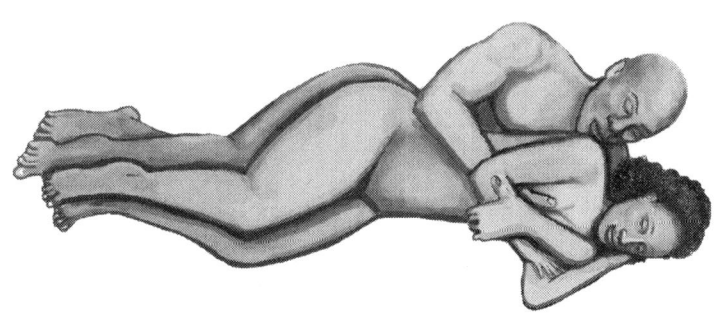

The Nurturer

June 22-July 22

Cancers, being the emotional creatures that they are, think that sex is an act of pure love. They either want to have a psychic experience with their lover or be nurtured and pampered in the process. These are the ones who need to feel comfortable and safe. And when they finally do, they may even try out the kitchen counter!

Symbol: The Crab
Ruling Planet: Moon
Body Part Ruled: Digestive system
House Ruled: Fourth, the house of the home
Element: Water
Color: Grey
Stone: Pearl
Key Phrase: I feel
Trait: Loyalty
Weakness: Manipulation
Quality: Cardinal

What Cancer Is All About

If I were a bumper sticker, it would say, "handle with care." My heart is very sensitive and I can't handle heartbreak. If you cause me any damage, you can be sure that this Cancer will find it impossible to forgive you. But please don't let that scare you. I'm a big nurturer. I would do anything to make sure my partner is happy. There is no doubt; if someone is looking for the ideal significant other, we're it. Sure, I might come across as a little shy, but don't be fooled. I like to get naughty.

Making people feel good about themselves is my greatest talent. I watch over my friends and hold them dear to my heart. I will be loyal for life to those who appreciate me and have my back. But I can always feel who my true friends are because I am so intuitive. Sometimes, I wish my intuition wasn't so strong because it hurts me when I know that someone doesn't really like me all that much. And I don't understand why not. Okay, so I can be moody and clingy sometimes, but what's wrong with that? If you don't feel secure, comforted, or loved, anybody would be moody. But I get over it.

I'm a great listener. I will listen to anyone's problems all day long and do my best to help in whatever way possible. I do my best to make them feel nurtured and loved. And what do you know? By helping others feel good, I feel good myself. All the moodiness disappears.

It's hard to share my deepest feelings and be completely open. I know that deep down I'm very strong and powerful, so there's no real reason to share any angst with anyone else. My emotions don't control me; I just tuck them away and use the energy for taking care of my family and friends. Some people think I'm a big mystery and don't understand me, but that's okay. I'm like the crab that comes out of its shell for a bit, and then scurries away and retreats back inside.

That's how I am; there's always a part of me that's hidden away. I'm very psychic and instinctive, so I know when it's time to hide beneath my shell to protect my heart. But this is also helpful for knowing who I can trust to be my romantic partner. I can see right through you, and if I don't feel good about your vibe, it's a no go.

Once I sense that you can be trusted, I'll throw off my shell and give you my heart. Sex for me is a deep, all-encompassing experience. I love lots of sweet foreplay to heighten all my senses, complete with the flittering candles, soft romantic music, fragrant flowers, and the feel of your skin against mine. It will be so sensuous, passionate, and unforgettable each and every time. I'm not the one to initiate something new because I'm shy about that. But I enjoy new experiences, so I'm willing to try whatever you want once I feel safe with you. And I'm all about pleasing you. Keeping you happy and satisfied is very exciting for me.

CANCER WOMAN:

The Cancer woman is the most natural homemaker, and the ideal for most men out there. A Cancer woman is someone who will take care of your home, your children, and you! But don't think that this woman is going to buy into that old "the only way to make a woman happy is to keep her barefoot and pregnant in the kitchen" school of thought. She is the ultimate nurturer of the zodiac, who loves her home, her mate, and her children. But she also works outside the home, and still finds the time to be a Domestic Goddess. And that balance is what makes her so sexy.

She likes compliments, but they have to be sincere, not just something to say to get her in between the sheets. A Cancer woman will respond much better to "you are so gorgeous" being whispered in her ear than any crass words, but not because she doesn't like sex, because she does, in fact, she loves it. She's just more excited by a gentler form of foreplay. She loves lots of kisses and goes for long make out sessions before anything else gets started.

The Cancer woman may feign resistance at a more aggressive move, but methinks the lady doeth protest too much. She will eventually respond to most advances, but only once this sensitive woman feels secure and knows her lover is trustworthy. She will be a loyal true blue, as long as her man is. If he's not, he'll be kicked out the door before he knows what hit him. Or, she may wait until she has revenge sex with someone else, just to show him that two can play that game. And then he'll be gone!

CANCER MAN:

The Cancer man is the most sensitive male lover of the zodiac, the one who puts the needs of his lover above those of his own. His sensitivity and tender nature is the stuff that can drive the ladies crazy. But this goes for the Cancer who is secure in his own skin, with his sexuality, and trusts his lover explicitly. If these things aren't in place, he may be a cranky, moody, jealous crab. His moods can wax and wane just like the Moon, which rules Cancer. This can be disconcerting because when he's on the mood swing highway, he can easily take his love interest along with him. Then if she gets too feisty, she'll send him scurrying back to that crusty shell.

When it comes to sex with no attachments, he's much more amenable to this than his female counterpart. While the female crab is looking for a romantic committed relationship, the male can separate his sensitive emotional side from his more practical one. This technique is really a means of protection from being hurt, but can make for a nice one-night stand.

If he finds a prospective mate, who is honest about her feelings towards him, can he then let go of his protective shell and be vulnerable? Yes. It's what he really wants and has been secretly looking for, but was afraid he'd never find. It will be perfect! He will be in 'til the end, and will go to the ends of the earth to make sure she's happy both in the bedroom and out. Making her happy will make him happy. While other signs like sex, or the release, the Cancer man *needs* it, *has* to have it, because that's what makes him feel secure in the relationship and their love. Then there's no more moody crab.

EROGENOUS ZONE:

The breast area for the Cancer woman and the chest for the Cancer Man are the most erogenous parts. Both love to be caressed in that area with light touches that lead to kissing and sucking on the nipples. Nibbling on the nipples is a really hot turn-on, as long it doesn't turn into full on biting.

SEX POSITION:

The Spoon. This is a perfect position for sex, or afterwards, when Cancer cuddles up to fall asleep. Fetishes include a passionate night in a luxury hotel, with some special things from home, maybe a scented candle, or a bundle of incense. But they'd be just as happy to stay home and have sex in a new part of the house.

SEX PROPS: Anything that can relax the cautious Cancer. A cocktail, a glass of wine, a toke, or whatever it takes so that Cancer can really let go and get into it!

Who Gets Them Hot And Not So Much

Hottest Sex: Taurus, Virgo, Scorpio, Pisces

One Night Stand (or Two): Cancer, Leo, Capricorn

Not So Much: Aries, Gemini, Libra, Sagittarius, Aquarius

Cancer with Aries:

Cancer and Aries are good for one, maybe two, hook ups. At first, it will seem exciting and they won't be able to get enough of each other, but after that, it just won't feel worth it. Cancer doesn't just like foreplay, but needs it. Aries' idea of foreplay is just thinking about sex. By the time Aries has his or her clothes off, it's action time, forget all the long kissing sessions just to begin Cancer's arousal. Cancer will just be getting into it, while Aries will be done and already snoozing. And outside the bedroom, they will mesh about as well as a Republican and Democratic in a heated debate!

Cancer with Taurus:

The seemingly slow natures of Cancer and Taurus wouldn't strike most people as being fertile ground for one of the greatest affairs of all time, but believe it or not, they'd be wrong. Slow and steady may not win the race for most, but this is one winning combo that can last for a lifetime. Both love security, comfort, their homes, and sex. While others are thinking that these two are boring, they will be moving through the house having sizzling sessions one room at a time. And that's just in one night. They will not care what anyone else thinks, and will just keep going at it. But this duo isn't just about the sex; they definitely know how to keep the romance going into matrimonial bliss.

Cancer with Gemini:

Cancer and Gemini will use sex as a competitive sport, and it will be exciting, for about five minutes. Gemini's wild "does anything" style will grab Cancer's interest and get them going. But by morning, Gem's wandering eye will open and be looking for the next conquest. This goes so against what the monogamy-loving Cancer wants that Gemini will find his or her hat being handed to them at the door. Any inkling of cheating is a big red flag for Cancer. Besides, Gemini thinks Cancer is too clingy and needy, so it would never work. So enjoy the good time, if there is any, and then move on!

Cancer with Cancer:

Cancer and Cancer are so alike they could be identical twins. They are so sensitive and so in tune with each other. At first, the sex will be delightful and so satisfying, because they intuitively know how to please each other in the same way they would want to be pleased themselves. It's like seeing their own reflections when looking in the mirror. The only problem is that the closer they look, the more flaws they see. Before long, they will be nipping at each other with those crab claws, as they are masters at pinching below the belt. This is when it's time to scurry on. The only good place for two crabs is at a New England Crab Boil on the beach.

Cancer with Leo:

Leo's lovemaking style can be a bit confusing for Cancer, but it need not be something to stop this union. Lions can be a bit full of themselves and slightly flamboyant, but there's no roving eye to be concerned about, like with the Gemini. Cancer will be drawn to how Leo stands by their chosen loved one. Leo will turn Cancer on to all sorts of sexy positions, some bordering on kinky, but as long as Cancer feels safe, there will be no problem. The only thing to prevent a lasting connection is that both the crab and the pussycat can be needy. As long as Cancer can keep Leo from turning into a big pussy, this could go from one-night stand to marriage material.

Cancer with Virgo:

Cancer and Virgo may not be the perfect combo right out of the gate, but if they work at it, it's going to be pretty close. Cancer loves being pampered and taken care of, and Virgo is just the one to do it, because they will do whatever it takes to make sure the other person is happy and satisfied. Virgo will analyze everything about Cancer's likes, dislikes, turn-ons, turn-offs, chart it out, and make a plan to keep Cancer completely happy. And Cancer will reciprocate to make sure all of Virgo's needs, wants, and desires in and out of the bedroom are taken care of.

Cancer with Libra:

The Moon, ruler of Cancer, and Venus, ruler of Libra, creates a match sent by the Gods. So Cancer and Libra should be fantastic too, right? No way in Hell. Don't even think about it, not even for one moment. If these two somehow managed to play any game of sex, they'd detest each other before either was declared the winner. Libra hates moody. And Cancer can't stand casual sex. This makes for one of the worst combos in the zodiac. Steer clear lest you commit mayhem.

Cancer with Scorpio:

Cancer and Scorpio are at the opposite end of the spectrum from Cancer and Libra. This combo is as good as that hot mess is bad. Cancer is possessive, Scorpio is intense, and they *love* when the two qualities mix. Scorpio will play with Cancer all day and all night, if that's what it takes for them to be pleased. It will definitely cure

Cancer's moody blues and alleviate any anger issues Scorpio might be battling. The Crab and Scorpion are in it for the "til death do we part" long haul!

Cancer with Sagittarius:

Sagittarius will take Cancer on an adventure full of memories that will last long after the excitement has worn off, and wear off it will. They will make better friends than lovers, even though there will be initial electricity flowing. When Cancer becomes needy and clingy, Sagittarius will be feeling antsy and start looking for freedom. If Sagittarius cheats, which is as likely to happen as the sun coming up tomorrow, Cancer will be pissed and kick them to the curb. So enjoy that one time, and just remain friends, before you take it to the point of no return.

Cancer with Capricorn:

This is a case of opposites attracting, with sparks flying from the get-go. Capricorn could wait for a lifetime to find the right person, and Cancer could be it. Cappy represents the Father of the zodiac, while Cancer is the Mother, so these two could make a nice little couple and procreate like daddies and mommies are meant to do. But after the first night of sex, the spark will flicker a little less bright, and will eventually burn out completely. Capricorn is more comfortable in the boardroom than the bedroom, and Cancer will get bored waiting for Cap to come home. This would never make it as love match.

Cancer with Aquarius:

This is one that probably won't even get off the ground, and if it does, who will even notice? The sex will be nothing to write home about or even think about. Aquarius is aloof and detached, which will annoy the hell out of Cancer. Cancer wants commitment and a loving relationship, and sex is what ties it all together for them. Emotional Cancer will have hurt feelings, while Aquarius will be wondering why, and won't be able to relate. It's just better to not get involved and avoid the inevitable. Too bad, but they can't all work out!

Cancer with Pisces:

This is another sexy match up, not as hot as Cancer and Scorpio, but almost. Both Cancer and Pisces are loving and devoted, when they trust each other. And both are supersensitive and know how to please the other. Cancer is nurturing, which is a big turn on for Pisces. Love making between these two will turn into a highly passionate affair that will totally blow both their minds. Outside of the bedroom, Cancer and Pisces are completely connected and can make a lifelong commitment. Cancer will take care of the mundane household duties, while Pisces will take care of the entertainment, especially the sexual kind.

Cancer Celebrities And Dirty, Sexy, Funny

Lizzy Caplan:

Lizzy Caplan has to know her way around the bedroom, at least on the little screen. In an interview with *LA Confidential*[18] she discussed being nominated for Best Actress in a Drama for her role in *Masters of Sex,* which depicts the real-life escapades of gynecologist, William Masters, and Virginia Johnson. These two teamed up to further Master's study of human sexuality. They quickly moved from a professional relationship to one that paralleled their research, and were married, for twenty-one years. Watching Lizzy in this role, you get the sense that she is just as sexually free as Virginia.

Sex and love go hand in hand for Cancers, especially the women. So it is only natural that Lizzy's character would fall for her partner in the study of sex. If Lizzy were in the same real life scenario, it would almost definitely play out the same for her.

Kevin Hart:

Kevin Hart may be short in stature, but when it comes to sex, he's at the top of the scale. His moves and body language show that he's at least a six or higher. That's a six on a one to five scale! On VladTV[19], his ex-wife backed that up when she said that he "put it down", and made her do crazy things. She didn't want anyone else to be getting any of his loving, so she had to put it down too!

The Cancer man can absolutely take charge anytime sex is involved, and knows all the right moves. So Kevin's ex was justified in thinking that all his moves would attract some other woman.

Benedict Cumberbatch:

Benedict Cumberbatch talked about sex in an interview with Elle UK[20], in which he was actually talking about sex and Sherlock Holmes, the character he plays for the BBC. The interviewer was quite adamant that Sherlock was a virgin and would be a horrible shag, if he were ever to take the plunge, but Benedict didn't agree on either fronts. He went on to say that Sherlock is a superb lover and knows exactly how to please a woman, even detailing how he would use his fingers and tongue in the act. He then stopped short to say he meant what Sherlock would do. Of course, to say all that he did, he has to know his way around a body. Or that boy has a very vivid imagination!

For a Cancer to respond so freely about sex, he has to be comfortable in his own sexuality, which is a big deal for Cancer. And Benedict did have to explain that he was talking about a role he played! Sounds like he was just trying to get the crab back in his shell!

Margot Robbie:

Margo Robbie told *US Magazine*[21] how she dominated Leonardo DiCaprio in her sex scene audition for the role of his wife in the *Wolf of Wall Street*. She said she was having a hard time keeping up and didn't know exactly what to do. Then, she decided to take a risk, and changed her scene directions, suddenly slapping him and telling him off, instead of just walking away. As a result, she was sure that not only would she not get the part, but she might also be sued in the process. She quickly apologized, but Leo thought it was brilliant and told her to hit him again. Of course she got the part and went on to sizzle in all the sex scenes on the big screen!

The female Cancer has a great sense of timing and reacts on her instincts. And Margot followed that instinct when she walloped Leo in her audition, which paid off brilliantly.

Jessica Simpson:

Jessica Simpson has always been open about her sex life, especially in her interview on *On-Air With Ryan Seacrest*[22]. She expounded on the delights of pregnancy and said she felt she couldn't be stopped in the bedroom. She then went on to tell Ryan how the Big O while pregnant was the Biggest O she ever had.

The Cancer woman oozes sexuality and is born to copulate. Just the fact that Jessica had some of her hottest sex while already pregnant is proof that she's a real Cancer woman.

Cancer Celebrity List

June 22:
Meryl Streep
Porsha Williams
Cyndi Lauper
Carson Daly
Kris Kristofferson
Kurt Warner
Bruce Campbell
Dan Brown

June 23:
Randy Jackson
Jason Mraz
Selma Blair
Clarence Thomas
Frances McDormand
Chet Faker
Aaron Ruell

June 24:
Solange Knowles
Mindy Kaling
Robert Downey Sr.
Minka Kelly
Mick Fleetwood
Jeff Beck
Peter Weller
Joe Penny

June 25:
George Michael
Ricky Gervais
Sonia Sotomayor
Carly Simon
Karisma Kapoor
Anthony Boudain
Kayleigh Pearson
Busy Philipps
Kellie Stewart

June 26:
Derek Jeter
Michael Vick
Amanda Cerny
Nick Offerman
Chris O'Donnell
Sean Hayes
Melanie Amaro
Mick Jones
Chris Isaak
Jason Scwartzman
Remy LaCroix

June 27:
Khloe Kardashian
Sam Claflin
Tobey Maguire

JJ Abrams
Cece Frey
Vera Wang
Christian Kane

June 28:
Kellie Pickler
John Elway
Kathy Bates
Mel Brooks
John Cusack
Steve Burton
Charlie Clapham
Bruce Davison
Michael Jacobs
Mary Stuart Masterson

June 29:
Nicole Scherzinger
Gary Busey
Neil Perry
Lily Rabe
Katherine Jenkins
Bret Mckenzie
Fred Gandy
Richard Lewis

June 30:
Mike Tyson
Michael Phelps
Fantasia Barrino

Lizzy Caplan
David Alan Grier
Rupert Graves
Monica Potter
James Martin

July 1:
Missy Elliott
Pamela Anderson
Liv Tyler
Dan Aykroyd
Deborah Harry
Claire Forlani
Carl Lewis
Serenay Sarikaya
Alan Ruck

July 2:
Ashley Tisdale
Lindsay Lohan
Margot Robbie
Larry David
Jose Canseco
Richard Petty
Jerry Hall
Michelle Branch
Johnny Weir
Sean Casey
Yancy Butler

July 3:
Tom Cruise
Thomas Gibson
Olivia Munn
Kurtwood Smith
Sandra Lee
Patrick Wilson
Audra McDonald
Connie Neilsen
Gloria Allred
Montel Williams
Moises Alou

July 4:
Mike The Situation
    Sorrentino
Alyssa Miller
Isabeli Fontana
Geraldo Rivera
Bill Withers
Andrew Zimmern
Carrie Keagan
Elie Saab
Finn Taylor

July 5:
Edie Falco
Eva Green
Chris Cline
Huey Lewis

Gilles Lellouche
Judge Joe Brown
Jenji Kohan
Kathryn Erbe
RZA
Zayed Khan
Terence Henricks

July 6:
Kevin Hart
50 Cent
Sylvester Stallone
Tia Mowry
Tamera Mowry
George W. Bush
Dalai Lama
Geoffrey Rush
Fred Dryer

July 7:
Ringo Starr
Kirsten Vangsness
Jim Gaffigan
Allen Payne
Michelle Kwan
Lisa Leslie
Jorga Fox
Kathryn McCormick
Billy Campbell
Toni Garrn

July 8:
Kevin Bacon
Sophia Bush
Toby Keith
Michael Weatherly
Beck
Milo Ventimiglia
Anjelica Huston
Rocky Carroll
Robert Knepper
Wolfgang Puck
Jeffrey Tambor
Billy Crudup

July 9:
Tom Hanks
Courtney Love
Jack White
Fred Savage
Nigel Lythgoe
Jimmy Smits
Enrique Murciano
John Tesh
Amanda Knox

July 10:
Sophia Vergara
Jessica Simpson
Adrian Grenier
Chiwetel Ejiofor

Alexandra Hedison
John Simm
Fiona Shaw
Arlo Guthrie
Roger Craig

July 11:
Lil Kim
Justin Chambers
John Henson
Cassi Davis
Richie Sambora
Lisa Rinna
Giorgio Armani
Sela Ward
Serinda Swan
Joan Smalls
Nadya Suleman
Dina Eastwood

July 12:
Michelle Rodriguez
Topher Grace
Loni Love
Cheryl Ladd
Richard Simmons
Kristi Yamaguchi
Anna Friel
Cheyenne Jackson

July 13:
Harrison Ford
Steven R. McQueen
Patrick Stewart
Ken Jeong
Cheech Marin
Spud Webb
Michael Spinks
Deborah Cox

July 14:
Jane Lynch
Peta Murgatroyd
Matthew Fox
Sara Canning
Tommy Mottola
Alex Perry
Jackie Earle Haley

July 15:
Gabriel Iglesias
Lana Parrilla
Arianna Huffington
Taylor Kinney
Forest Whitaker
Linda Ronstadt
Diane Kruger
Brian Austin Green
Eddie Griffin
Scott Foley
Terry O'Quinn

July 16:
Will Ferrell
Barry Sanders
Corey Feldman
Jimmy Johnson
Phoebe Cates
Michael Flatley
Ruben Blades

July 17:
Luke Bryan
David Hasselhoff
Donald Sutherland
Camilla Parker Bowles
Jason Clarke
Tony Dovolani
Gino D'Acampo
Lucie Arnaz
Mark Burnett
Diahann Carroll
Sarah Jones
Robin Shou
Geezer Butler

July 18:
Vin Diesel
Kristen Bell
Chace Crawford
Wendy Williams
Jim Bob Duggar
MIA

Richard Branson
John Glenn
Ricky Skaggs
James Brolin
Kelly Reilly
Martha Reeves

July 19:
Benedict Cumberbatch
Chris Kratt
Campbell Scott
Rosie Jones
Angela Griffin
Vinessa Shaw
Nancy Carell
Lisa Lampanelli
Jim Norton

July 20:
Julianne Hough
Gisele Bundchen
Carlos Santana
Omar Epps
Sandra Oh
Josh Holloway
Chris Cornell
Dwayne Wayans
Judy Greer
Leah Miller
Donna Dixon

July 21:
Robin Williams
Josh Hartnett
Deandre Jordan
Sara Sampaio
Cat Stevens
Rory Culkin
Chelsie Hightower
Ali Landry
Jon Lovitz
Brandi Chastain
Ariel Meredith

July 22:
Selena Gomez
David Spade
AJ Cook
Danny Glover
Alex Trebek
Willem Dafoe
Don Henley
John Leguizamo
Oscar de la Renta
Rhys Ifans
Albert Brooks
Keyshawn Johnson
Rob Estes

EO

July 23 – August 22

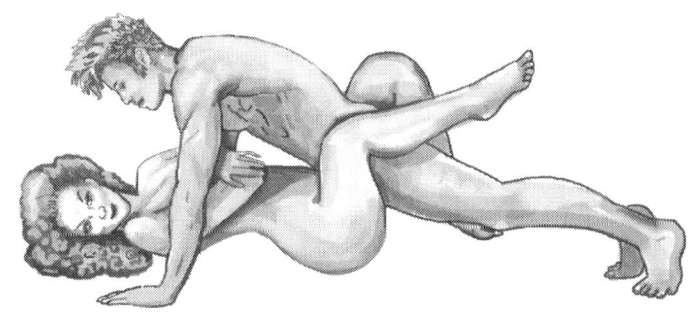

The Leader

July 23-August 22

Leo can't be matched when it comes to passion and adventure. They use their great imagination and creative skills to find new sexual techniques that impress even themselves. But they're not too selfish. Leo does bring his or her partner along for the ride.

Symbol: Lion
Ruling Planet: Sun
Body Part Ruled: Heart
House Ruled: Fifth. The house of creativity, romance, and children
Element: Fire
Color: Gold
Stone: Ruby
Key Phrase: I will
Trait: Creative
Weakness: Arrogance
Quality: Fixed

What Leo Is All About

If there were a celebrity billboard attached to the Hollywood sign, it would have my picture on it. I am the star of my own real life play and live center stage for my audience. A following of fans that appreciate me, adore me, and put me on a pedestal is really important to me. That way I don't feel alone; I can't stand to be alone. That's the worst feeling ever.

But that doesn't mean I'm needy or dependent. I just like having people around as long as they don't try to be the boss of me. I hate to be told what to do. It's one thing that can be a deal breaker. I just have to say, "Bye, bye! You're outa here!"

I am the greatest friend; all my friends will say so. They are drawn to me like a moth to a flame. With all my fiery energy, I can understand why. I'm so enthusiastic about life; everyone wants to be around me. Who wouldn't want to be? Since I'm the social butterfly of the zodiac, I'll usually be found flitting from one adorning fan to the next, as they huddle around me at any big soiree. It's difficult for people to not like me, that's how likeable I am. I am generous with my friends, and indulge them with all the little, and big, things that they desire.

Some people think I'm self-centered, and I know I can be. But sometimes I just have to focus on what I want to do with my life and my desires. But if anyone needs me, I'll drop everything in a flash and be right there with anything they need. I'm never so self-absorbed that I can't be helpful or there for people. Some catty people would say I only do it for the attention, but I don't give a rip what they say. Yes, there are times I do things to be noticed, I'll be the first to admit it, but not when I'm helping others.

Ordinary, dreary routines drive me up the wall. If I can't have remarkable and amazing, I'll stir up some shit just to get my blood pumping. I am so sensitive, but you'd never know, because I keep it well hidden. I can get my feelings hurt, which makes me so unhappy. An unhappy Lion isn't a good thing to be around, trust me; I don't even like myself when that happens. So I'll do anything it takes to turn back into a purring pussycat.

People think that I'm into kink in the bedroom, but not so much. I show my partners some variety as long as I am familiar with what we're doing, and because I pride myself on being the best. If you have something in mind that I've never tried, I'd want to pass until I learn more about it. I like everything to be perfect when getting down to it, rather than attempting it and coming up short, pun intended. My moves are awesome and I have them all down pat. I won't disappoint with what I do. I will make sure there's lots of together time. I am very good, in fact. I am the best, if I say so myself!

LEO WOMAN:

The Leo woman is a flirt and a tease. And her making any first moves is fairly rare. It's all about the chase, you chasing her. If her coquettish ways aren't enough to spark your interest, she'll find a man who's prompt to respond to her wiles. Does that mean she's the unfaithful type? Not as long as you put her on the pedestal she thinks deserves.

She has a streak of vanity that has to be appeased and admired. The saying "flattery will get you anywhere" was probably written about a Leo woman. That's the quickest way to get to her and have her purring like a kitten. But remember, she's not a lap cat, she's the Queen of the Jungle and will follow her primal instincts when it comes to sex. Once she has her claws into you, she'll call the bedroom shots however the mood strikes her. Whatever she wants, she's going to get!

She wants to be adored and have her body worshipped; and will put on a tantalizing show for you with all the lights on. No sex in the dark for her. Not even just flickering candles. No, she wants enough light so you can see everything and tell her how beautiful her body is. That gets her libido going before any sexual contact is made. This is a woman with big expectations. She wants her freedom to be admired by every male who sees her, not that she will accept advances from any of them; she simply loves having all eyes on her. But she expects you to only have eyes for her. Once this is established, she'll be willing to experiment when it comes to sex, much more so than the male Leo. She thinks if something feels good, she should just do it. She'll want to know how you know it doesn't feel good if you've never tried it. Then she'll be willing to break out all the stops, as well as all the toys, to give it a try. If she doesn't like something, at least she's going to know why.

LEO MAN:

Just as the Leo woman is susceptible to flattery, the Leo man buys into admiration big time, almost to the point of it being his downfall. He can get so caught up in the accolades and adulation that he doesn't realize that she may not be the one for him. When he is blinded by narcissism, he could find himself in a sticky wicket if he thinks it's the perfect catch without bypassing his ego, and checking in with his real feelings. He really is a man's man, robust and masculine, but can easily fall prey to a woman who knows how to wrap him around her little finger.

He can easily fall in love and wonders why it doesn't last. He has grand ideas about what he thinks romantic love should be that don't quite match reality. Leo can be really full of himself with that great big ego, and can get on some people's nerves once in a while. But he certainly can keep people entertained at social events. They will flock around him, completely enamored by his charisma.

Some people think he is the non-emotional King, but deep down, he is highly sensitive, and best suited for a woman who not only knows how to please him, but will also do it willingly. He's not the demanding sort, but he does have a sense of entitlement. Since he's so great, he deserves to be treated accordingly. He will make sure his lover gets hers in the bedroom, but you will hear him roar when he hits his stride.

EROGENOUS ZONE:

Just like a domestic tabby, this big cat loves being petted with long strokes down the back. Leo will even go for some light scratching as long as you don't break the skin. A full back massage may have other signs relaxed and dozing off, but it gets Leo ready for a *real* petting session.

SEX POSITION:

She, on her back with knees bent, one foot on bed other on his back, while he does "push-ups", the hard kind, no bent knees for him! Fetishes that can intrigue Leo are having sex on the beach, or doing a strip tease; they love exhibitionism!

SEX PROPS:

Leo adores themselves and their own bodies, so a camera is the perfect item for getting them hot. They also like a good game of Strip Poker, so you can snap some shots to document the progress. Then be sure take a photo of the winner. In this case, it's the one who gets naked first!

Who Gets Them Hot And Not So Much

Hottest Sex: Aries, Gemini, Leo, Libra, Sagittarius

One Night Stand (or Two): Cancer, Virgo, Scorpio, Aquarius

Not So Much: Taurus, Capricorn, Pisces

Leo with Aries:

Sex between Leo and Aries is H-O-T! Set the house on fire hot. These two fire signs go for it in and out of the bedroom; no slow sensual movements for them. They'll get downright freaky if left to their own devices. Trapeze bar, dance pole, you name it, they're willing to give it a try. Things can get heated between Leo and Aries when they don't agree. Both like all the attention, which can lead to some serious fights, but the making up is over the top. This will turn in to a long-term match, if they can learn to share the spotlight, or at least take turns.

Leo with Taurus:

Leo struts around like the king of the jungle and Taurus thinks it's all bullshit. Leo wants to be in charge, and Taurus doesn't want to be bossed around, at least not by the Lion. What about the sex? There probably won't be any. Taurus thinks Leo has a roving eye like Gemini and Sagittarius, which gets a huge "nothing for you" from the Bull. Leo will spend a bundle to have fun, and thinks Taurus is a tight ass. Both are stubborn and dig their heels in to the point of not budging an inch. Unless they are into ironclad prenups, they shouldn't take the walk to the I-dos. Better yet, they should just say, "I don't" in the beginning.

Leo with Gemini:

When Leo and Gemini meet up for a quick drink, it may turn into a quickie instead, because they won't be able to keep their hands off each other and don't really care if anyone else notices. And that's okay because both are show offs at heart, which pretty much means they are up for anything. Not that Leo and Gemini go for public displays of nudity, but close to it. They go all out to make sure they both are happy. The only thing that can keep this from being a lasting union is if Gemini can't remain true blue to the Lion. No one cheats on the Lion!

Leo with Cancer:

Leo and Cancer are both romantics; believe in the power of love and good sex. But the approach is totally different.

For Leo, sex is a party, a celebration with them at the center of it all, being adored and fawned over. Cancer wants the personal intimacy where they can bare their soul. While Leo will be thrilled with all the attention that Cancer gives, the Lion's constant need for praise will soon irritate the Crab. Likewise, Cancer will initially be turned on by Leo's huge bag of tricks and positions, but will then be turned off when Leo is more interested in themself than taking care of Cancer's needs. If they are to get together at all, it won't be for anything long-term.

Leo with Leo:

Two regal beasts in one bed is one too many. Each wants to be the King or Queen of his or her own jungle. Both Leos want to be the main attraction at the same time. Leo number one will say, "Run those nails up and down my back," while Leo number two will say, "Hell no, you scratch my back!" While it's not a physical impossibility for this to happen simultaneously, neither can put the focus on the other because they each want the universe to revolve around them. So spats begin, which easily turn into full on arguments. This overflows out of the bedroom, into the rest of life, and they are soon bickering about whose turn it is to take out the garbage. If they could just compromise, this could be the best dance of their lives. But most Lions never back off from anything.

Leo with Virgo:

The Leo/Virgo combo can be a great one-night stand because anybody can stand almost anything for a short period of time. But taking it any further than that will be too much to bear, for Virgo at least. Leo will fall for Virgo's intelligent mind, but feel that the sex is way too tame. Leo's bedroom antics and attitudes can make Virgo blush, or back off in disgust. Away from the bedroom, Virgo is driven up the wall by Leo's obsessive need for attention, and Leo thinks Virgo is a bossy know-it-all. They have no real chance to make a go of it, so split before it gets ugly.

Leo with Libra:

Libra thinks love and sex is a romantic and exciting mental adventure, while Leo has a more physical let's-get-it-on attitude. But with a few communication tweaks, this works for them. Libra can be wishy-washy when making decisions about almost everything. Leo loves to be in charge, so it is a win-win situation. Leo's charisma and larger than life persona will keep Libra intrigued. Both are extravagant, so they'll need to watch how much they spend, but whether this combo ends up as the prince or the pauper, they'll have a rich sex life.

Leo with Scorpio:

Brilliant, beautiful fireworks start the minute Leo and Scorpio lay eyes on each other. Sex will be hotter than hot! For the faint-of-heart, it would be the beginning of the usual love story, Boy loves Girl, Girl loves Boy, shit happens, and it's all over but the shouting. But that is the end of usual when it comes to these two, because things will just be beginning to HEAT up. There can be issues; Scorpio will think Leo is way too friendly, when it's just the outgoing nature of the beast, and Leo wonders why Scorpio doesn't worship the ground those kitty paws walk on 24/7. But none of this is serious enough to keep them out of each other's arms. Or make that paws and claws! A couple of differences only make it all the more interesting!

Leo with Sagittarius:

Leo and Sagittarius both love having fun. Together, this pair can generate plenty of heat. Leo has a good bedroom repertoire, but Sagittarius conjures up a trick or three that will have this big cat purring and begging for a back scratch. Leo likes to be on center stage and Sag will gladly sit back and watch. The only problem is that while both seem to not have a jealous bone, Sagittarius has roaming tendencies, which are apt to make Leo growl a bit. So Leo will have to step it up a notch to keep Sag entertained.

Leo with Capricorn:

Both Leo and Capricorn like lots of sex, and to be in control. Leo loves spontaneity, while Capricorn plans every detail. Capricorn may rule with an iron fist in the boardroom, but trying to be the boss of Leo will cause more rebellion than the KatyCats at a sold out Katy Perry concert. Capricorn boys and girls have an instinctive distrust and disdain for Leos, seeing them as capricious, impetuous, and childish. This isn't good for sustaining even a hot one-night stand; it would be lukewarm at best.

Leo with Aquarius:

Opposites attract when Leo and Aquarius meet up. The Aquarius demeanor is intriguing to Leo, who wants to get through that cool exterior to reach the *real* Aquarius. Imagine Leo's surprise when realizing that what you see is what you get with Aquarius; their altruistic nature is the real deal. Leo loves going to parties and socializing with the best of them, while Aquarius would rather head for the bar and avoid all the frivolity. While they could have a couple steamy sessions in bed, this isn't one for the long term.

Leo with Pisces:

No good can come from the Leo and Pisces pairing. Leo lives firmly on terra firma, while Pisces has his or her head in the clouds. Leo wants a real flesh and blood sexual interaction, and Pisces wants the ethereal experience. Unless they both have a really good buzz going on, they're not likely to make it to first base, let alone the real action. Just leave it alone, and remember that the only time Cats love Fish is when they find them in their bowl at dinnertime.

Leo Celebrities And Dirty, Sexy, Funny

Jennifer Lawrence:

In an interview with Conan O'Brien, Jennifer Lawrence spilled the beans on a recent scandal in her life![23] She told about how the hotel housekeeping staff found a profuse supply of sex toys in a box under the bed in her room. She alleged that they were a gag gift from a friend. Would have been a good opportunity to give some of them a go! Hmmm!

Confident describes the Leo woman perfectly. Jennifer displayed confidence in spades in comfortably telling Conan all about the stash of toys, especially for the whole world to hear.

Madonna:

When interviewed for *The Advocate*[24], Madonna was asked if she uses any type of sex toys. She replied that she's never owned any artificial sexual enhancers, and that it's all about the living breathing body. She indicated that fingers could work just as well as vibrators.

The personality of the Leo woman is that of a real straight shooter, and Madonna certainly lives up to that reputation. Never one to back away from letting the public know what's on her mind, she tells it like it is.

Jennifer Lopez:

Andy Cohen knew how to get down to the nitty-gritty when he interviewed Jennifer Lopez on *Watch What Happens Live*[25]. He got her to say that what she really desires in a man is someone who is tender and kind, and will make her laugh, rather than someone who is just hot. She went on to say that she's not in to good looks, and doesn't think looks equate with sexiness. After almost rolling with laughter, Andy got her to confess that her most daring place to have sex was on a hotel balcony, but her lips were sealed on when the who and where.

Leo woman has a great sense of humor, usually accompanied by a distinctive laugh. So the fact that Jennifer wants someone who can bring the giggles, ties into that. But since most of the guys she has dated have been attractive, some downright gorgeous, looks must come to play a little bit.

Antonio Banderas:

Antonio Banderas got his U. S. film start in Madonna's *Truth or Dare,* playing the object of her attention. He talked in *Harper's Bazaar*[26] about how he didn't understand what it meant when someone told him that Madonna liked him, a lot. He went on to say that he turned down her advances. In *Biography Magazine*[27], he dispelled all the rumors that he and Angelina Jolie actually had sex in *Original Sin*. He also doesn't get what all the hype is about his Latin Lover reputation. Obviously, he's never watched those steamy scenes from *Original Sin* or the ones with Salma Hayek in *Desperado*.

Being in the spotlight is exactly what Leos adore, so even though Antonio sounds modest, he is right where he's meant to be!

Leo Celebrity List

July 23:
Daniel Radcliffe
Woody Harrelson
Marlon Wayans
Michelle Williams
Monica Lewinsky
Alison Krauss
Gary Payton
Tristan MacManus
Stephanie Seymour
Stephanie March
Bill Chott

July 24:
Kristin Chenoweth
Anna Paquin
Rose Byrne
Barry Bonds
Rick Fox
Karl Malone
Summer Glau
Eric Szmanda
Gallagher
John Aniston
Elizabeth Moss
Chris Sarandon

July 25:
Matt LeBlanc
Iman Abdulmajid
Conor Kennedy
Lil Phat
Michael Welch
Kevin McCall
DB Woodside
Geoffrey Zakarian
David Denman

July 26:
Elizabeth Gillies
Sandra Bullock
Jason Statham
Mick Jagger
Taylor Momsen
Kate Beckinsale
Kevin Spacey
Helen Mirren
Joe Jackson
Dorothy Hamill
Jeremy Piven
Ana Patricia Gonzalez
Chris Harrison
Deepika Singh
Olivia Williams

July 27:
Triple H
Alex Rodriguez
Maya Rudolph
Taylor Schilling
Seamus Dever
Jonathan Rhys Meyers
Julian McMahon
Bill Engvall
Peggy Fleming
Christopher Dean
Roxanne Hart

July 28:
Lori Loughlin
Manu Ginobili
Jim Davis
Elizabeth Berkley
Sally Struthers
Dulquer Salmaan
Dustin Milliga
Billy Aaron Brown

July 29:
Josh Radnor
Fernando Alonso
Paulina Goto
Martina McBride
Wil Wheaton
Tim Gunn
Elizabeth Dole

Stephen Dorff
Alexandra Paul
Danger Mouse

July 30:
Arnold Schwarzenegger
Lisa Kudrow
Terry Crews
Hope Solo
Simon Baker
Vivica A. Fox
Tom Green
Christopher Nolan
Hilary Swank
Alton Brown
Laurence Fishburne
Gina Rodriguez
Jaime Pressly
Paul Anka
Jean Reno
Frank Stallone
Elvis Crespo
Delta Burke

July 31:
JK Rowling
Wesley Snipes
AJ Green
Charlie Carver
Mark Cuban
Zac Brown

Demararcus Ware
Zelda Williams
Dean Cain
BJ Novak
Michael Biehn

August 1:
Bobby Shmurda
Max Carver
Coolio
Tempestt Bledsoe
Jack O'Connell
Madison Bumgarner
Jason Momoa
Roy Williams
Van Vicker
Elijah Kelley
Robert Cray
Adam Duritz
Rampage

August 2:
Charli XCX
Sam Worthington
Dingdong Dantes
Mary Louise Parker
Edward Furlong
Kevin Smith
Wes Craven
Victoria Jackson
Angelica Rivera

Isabel Allende
Apollonia Kotero

August 3:
Tom Brady
Michael Ealy
Evangeline Lilly
Karlie Kloss
Martha Stewart
Tony Bennett
Martin Sheen
Jourdan Dunn
Isaiah Washington
Melissa Ponzio
John C. McGinley
Mamie Gummer
John Landis

August 4:
Barack Obama
Dylan Sprouse
Cole Sprouse
Jeff Gordon
Billy Bob Thornton
Daniel Dae Kim
Lee Mack
Meghan Markle
Sebastian Roche
Richard Belzer
Crystal Chappell

August 5:
Jesse Williams
Lolo Jones
Maureen McCormick
Patrick Ewing
Loni Anderson
DeRay Davis
Pete Burns
J Ax

August 6:
Geri Halliwell
Vera Farmiga
Soleil Moon Frye
Marisa Miller
David Robinson
Tre Mason
Michelle Yeoh
Catherine Hicks
M Night Shyamalan
Melissa George
Michael Parr

August 7:
Charlize Theron
David Duchovny
Francesca Eastwood
Samantha Ronson
Tobin Bell
Michael Shannon
Wayne Knight

Garrison Keillor
Harold Perrineau

August 8:
Meagan Good
Roger Federer
Dustin Hoffman
Princess Beatrice
Connie Stevens
Jen Selter
Mel Tillis
Drew Lachey
Donnie Most
Larry Wilcox
Robin Quivers

August 9:
Anna Kendrick
Young Thug
Deion Sanders
Sam Elliott
Michael Kors
Gillian Anderson
Eric Bana
Jessica Capshaw
Melanie Griffith
Kevin McKidd
Hoda Kotb
Audrey Tautou
Bill Skarsgard

August 10:
Antonio Banderas
Angie Harmon
Betsey Johnson
Justin Theroux
Devon Aoki
Rosanna Arquette
Rhonda Fleming

August 11:
Chris Hemsworth
Hulk Hogan
Pablo Sandoval
Viola Davis
Steve Wozniak
Embeth Davidtz
Anna Gunn
Sophie Okonedo
Chris Messina

August 12:
Cara Delevingne
Cher Coulter
Imani Hakim
Anthony Ray
Casey Affleck
Dominique Swaim
Pete Sampras
Bruce Greenwood
Michael Ian Black
Peter Krause

August 13:
Fidel Castro
Mo
DeMarcus Cousins
Danny Bonaduce
Debi Mazar
Bobby Clarke
Koji Kondo
John Slattery

August 14:
Mila Kunis
Halle Berry
Tim Tebow
Earvin Magic Johnson
Steve Martin
Catherine Bell
Lady Bunny
Sarah Brightman
David Crosby
Danielle Steel
Connie Smith
Marcia Gay Harden
Jennifer Flavin

August 15:
Jennifer Lawrence
Joe Jonas
Ben Affleck
Anthony Anderson
Debra Messing

Natasha Henstridge
Melinda Gates
Cris Judd
David Zayas
Tom Colicchio

August 16:
Madonna
Steve Carell
Angela Bassett
James Cameron
Kathie Lee Gifford
Timothy Hutton
Rumer Willis
Frank Gifford

August 17:
Robert De Niro
Paula Bel
Taissa Farmiga
Mark Sailing
Donnie Wahlberg
Larry Ellison
Sean Penn
Giuliana Rancic
Mae West

August 18:
Andy Samberg
Edward Norton
Robert Redford

Frances Bean Cobain
Christian Slater
Patrick Swayze
Denis Leary
Madeleine Stowe
Martin Mull
Mika Boorem
Rosalynn Carter

August 19:
John Stamos
Matthew Perry
Bill Clinton
Fat Joe
Kyra Sedgwick
Jonathan Frakes
Peter Gallagher
Tracie Thoms
Erika Christensen
Lee Ann Womack

August 20:
Demi Lovato
Amy Adams
Robert Plant
Al Roker
James Marsters
Fred Durst
Don King
Connie Chung
John Noble

August 21:
Hayden Panettiere
Brad Kavanagh
Brody Jenner
Kenny Rogers
Loretta Devine
Kim Cattrall
Carrie Anne Moss
Alicia Witt
Jim Mcmahon

August 22:
Ty Burrell
Kristen Wiig
Richard Armitage
Giada De Laurentiis
Tori Amos
Valerie Harper

VIRGO

August 23 – September 22

The Analyst

August 23-September 22

Virgo has the appearance of being prim and proper, but give them a stack of condoms and a neatly made bed with clean sheets, and that reserved façade melts away. They just don't walk around showing their inner lustiness. These are the people who carry the romp from the bedroom to soaping each other down in the shower!

Symbol: The Virgin
Ruling Planet: Mercury
Body Part Ruled: Nervous system
House Ruled: Sixth, the house of health and service
Element: Earth
Color: Navy Blue
Stone: Sapphire
Key Phrase: I analyze
Trait: Conscientiousness
Weakness: Criticalness
Quality: Mutable

What Virgo Is All About

Analytical is a word that really describes me. And I am very intelligent. The combination of these two helps me get things done. I'm a doer and can get to the bottom of any problem. If you need any issues in your life ferreted out, I'm the person to call.

I have a great memory and scientific mind, which helps me see into and through people, to see what their motives are. This is both a blessing and a curse; it's a blessing because I can help investigators or regular people solve problems. But it can be a curse when I'm romantically involved with someone. Just when I think I can trust them, I can sense what's really going, and discover they're not being faithful or upfront.

Some would think this would also be a blessing, and in some ways it really is, but it's hurtful. I don't just give my heart to anyone on a whim. I sit back and analyze everything, and tune in to my intuition before I even decide I'm going to take a chance on love. I don't go into it lightly, so I'm sure that what I know about my lover is real at the time, that there's no hidden agenda. That's what makes it so disappointing when things change.

I don't like change; I like it to be status quo. Everything has to be neat and tidy, organized, a place for everything and everything in its place. This includes my mind. I like to have my thoughts all organized and compartmentalized; but it's a tough thing to do. My mind never shuts off, more thoughts and ideas just keep popping in.

Some people, okay almost everyone, thinks I'm anal. I don't mean to be a control freak or anally retentive, but I can't help it. My memory banks won't allow me to let go of anything. If I could just get out of my head and into my feelings, I'd be okay, no, I'd be great. But the one thing I don't want to analyze is my feelings.

When I trust a person enough to be intimate with them, I'm really hot in bed. I love sex, lots of it. I may not have a lot of moves or know a lot of positions, but I make up for it in tenacity. I won't initiate something new, but if you do, I'm willing to try it out, at least once. Of course, then I'll do an analysis, weigh the pros and cons, and decide if it's worth doing again.

As time goes on, and I'm really secure in our relationship, I'll relax and all my pent up hotness will burst out. Every time will be more and more sensual and pleasurable than the last.

If you catch me being too in my head when you're ready to rock my world, go for my tummy. My whole tummy is so sensitive. You can start by just rubbing my tummy, even with my clothes on. Once you get me out of them, start tracing big circles on my skin, getting smaller and smaller, until they're tiny circles around my navel. That drives me crazy! I'll be outta my mind and into my body in a flash, ready for you to take me places I've never been before!

VIRGO WOMAN:

Many think that the Virgo woman is a prude, but there's a big difference between a prude and a lady. Extremely intelligent, with a very analytical mindset, she does well in the business world. She can turn your failing company right around with all her analytical savvy. But when she comes home, gets out of her suit, and takes her hair down, watch out!

She's a sexual hottie, who will keep it under wraps until the right person comes around. It's not obvious that she's so into sex; in fact, she may come across as being detached and cold. It may take a little, or a lot of patience, and it will definitely take some heavy wooing. But once you get under that cool reserved surface, you'll find the heart of a real woman. Get her going and she'll definitely keep up with you, maybe even give you a run for your money.

It isn't just love and sex she's after; she wants the partnership, but has been protecting her heart for a long time. Once you get her to fall in love with you, she knows you're one to be trusted; it's for keeps. Devotion and loyalty are the words she lives by. She will love making you happy.

Just remember that she needs to be stimulated intellectually as well as physically. It goes beyond needing, it's a tonic and restorative for her. That may be the one area that would cause her to seek something outside the walls of her domain. She would much rather be at home with you discussing things that interest her. So don't give her a reason to feel useless or unfulfilled. Listen to the news, buy a book, be informed, and she'll fulfill all your wildest dreams!

VIRGO MAN:

The Virgo man is very cool on the outside and very sensitive on the inside. He can be a hard nut to crack, since he plays his emotions so close to the vest. It takes understanding and patience, a lot of patience, to get close to him. If you try to get in to his psyche too soon, he will feel threatened and retreat even further. He struggles to let his feelings out, but really tries, which often creates unintentional conflict for him and his lover.

This man has to have a classy lady who is conventional, rational, and doesn't do things impulsively. He is predictable and, like his female counterpart, doesn't like change. He wants a woman who is the same, one he can count on to have his back and allow him to feel safe and secure when he comes home. No one else will ever see this vulnerable side to him, so he has to be able to trust the woman he gives his heart to with no reservations.

He may not be the sweep-you-off-your-feet guy when you first get together, but that can come later. He won't leave your side and will be loyal beyond words. When you break through his protective walls, you'll unleash a sexual fireball. Unlike some of the hound dogs of the zodiac, he's an equal opportunity guy; in other words, he gives as good as he gets, and will want you right there with him when the rockets blast off.

If you want romance and flowers, just let him know, then be patient and don't nag. Don't worry; you'll never have to mention it again. He may have a stubborn streak, but when it comes to making you happy, he'll learn what you like, store it away in his huge memory, and surprise you when you least expect it.

EROGENOUS ZONE:

The entire stomach area is sensitive for Virgo. They'll respond to anything from light tickles to a soapy massage followed by a misty water spray!

SEX POSITION:

A modified scissors where great eye contact is involved!

SEX PROPS:

This is a sex game! Write down 5 wildly erotic sex acts on separate pieces of paper, throw them in a bowl, bag, hat, or whatever you have handy, have Virgo pull one out, and do what it says. Spontaneity is a huge turn on for Virgo, especially since they're typically so predictable!

Who Gets Them Hot And Not So Much

Hottest Sex: Taurus, Cancer, Virgo, Scorpio, Capricorn

One Night Stand (or Two): Gemini, Aquarius

Not So Much: Aries, Leo, Libra, Sagittarius, Pisces

Virgo with Aries:

Take-charge Aries will get away with telling Virgo what to do a couple of times. After that, Virgo catches on to the Aries M.O. of leaping and then looking, and decides they're out. Virgo will stop listening, and Aries, the authority on everything, sexual or not, will get pissed. There's pretty much no coming back from this scenario, even if they ever made it to the bedroom in the first place.

Virgo with Taurus:

Instead of being a match made in Heaven, it's one made right here on Earth. These two Earth signs are made for each other. Physically, they mesh in all the right places. The Bull can have the Virgin in the mood quicker than most of the other signs Virgo connects with, even though Taurus takes it nice and slow. It's because of that slow approach, and the Taurus' willingness to please, that the Virgo is so intrigued. If they ever make it out of the bedroom, which will take effort, Virgo will analyze everything to make sure they are safe and secure, and Taurus will stash funds away for their future. The chances of these two not making it are as likely as Warren Buffet losing his billions.

Virgo with Gemini:

Virgo and Gemini are both ruled by Mercury, which gives them incredible skills when it comes to talking, but that's part of the problem. They would much rather have fun talking about sex together, than actually doing the act. Virgo needs intense passionate contact, while Gemini is into making a game of it. Their style of talking, which reflects on their real personalities, creates other problems. Gem is a big gossip, while Virgo wants to talk about their relationship goals, which causes Virgo to think Gemini is an ignorant jerk and Gemini to think Virgo is a boring jackass! Better they stay with friendly chats as friends.

Virgo with Cancer:

This could be the opportunity for an enjoyable quick affair, but that isn't likely because these two both like going for the relationship experience. The sex will be great between them, so they'll have a stellar beginning. Cancer wants a stable partner who will stick around through thick and thin, and Virgo will gladly step up to the plate and assume the position. Virgo wants someone who will worship the ground they walk on, and when Cancer surrenders his or her heart, that is exactly what they do!

Virgo with Leo:

This is one that should be left alone as Leo's ideas on sex don't coincide with Virgo's. For Virgo, sex is full of sensual, mental, and physical exchanges. Leo thinks sex is a daily necessity like food and water. Leo will make absurd romp requests that Virgo will find hilarious and a major turn off. The Lion thinks he or she is the supreme ruler of all they see, while Virgo thinks it's so much cat shit. After Virgo bursts Leo's inflated ego, they'll just walk away from the disaster.

Virgo with Virgo:

Thinking alike is even more pronounced between two mental Virgos. They'll be totally in sync on everything, whether it's discussing Buddhist meditation, or where to have dinner. Could this be an issue? Only if they let it, which isn't likely, unless they both go into critical mode and start taking jabs at each other. Physical contact will get them out of their heads and into the sensuous feelings in their bodies. One of Virgo's greatest assets is dedication to service, and they will definitely take turns serving each other during blissful nights or days.

Virgo with Libra:

Initially, this is a combo for some spicy sex. Libra can attract Virgo unimaginably with his or her sizzling allure. Virgo likes possessing their sexual partners, and Libra willingly obliges. So what goes wrong? Libra is one of the social butterflies of the zodiac, and wants to party down and spend all his or her cash having a good time. Virgo's idea of a good time is staying at home, making dinner, having sex, watching a movie, and going off to bed, not necessarily in that order. To Libra, this sounds boring as hell. Virgo's critical tongue will give Libra a thrashing and then there's no more spice to the sex!

Virgo with Scorpio:

This is one of the best unions in the zodiac in all areas, bedroom or not! Both signs have issues with trust, but once they are past that, and know they can confide in each other, it's all up hill from there. Scorpio's passion sets free any of Virgo's hidden sexual desires, which is incredible for both of them. Virgo relinquishes their usual need to be in control and allows Scorpio to call all the shots. This results in staying in bed for days at a time with the food delivery service on speed dial. Outside the bedroom, Scorpio makes sure Virgo feels safe and secure, while Virgo's adoration makes Scorpio ecstatic.

Virgo with Sagittarius:

Lots of times, opposites attract and go way beyond that, ending up as the couple of the century. Virgo and

Sagittarius? No way, no how! These two most likely can't even stand each other enough to be acquaintances, let alone friends. And lovers or sex partners? Forget it! Hate is such a strong word, but how about repulsion or repugnance. That pretty much sums up what they feel for each other. Imagine the Dalai Lama matched up with Courtney Love, and you have an idea about the chances for Virgo and Sagittarius getting together. Did someone say a snowball's chance in hell? No need to even talk about the sex, 'cause there won't be any!

Virgo with Capricorn:

You would think Virgo and Capricorn were two Fire signs instead of Earth, that's how much heat they will generate. These two are supposed to be shy and reserved, but they'd better keep a fire extinguisher close by in case they set the bedroom on fire. Once they share their fantasies with each other, they may have to invest in a whole wardrobe of costumes for roleplaying. The sex will be fantastic. They may end up being the real life princess and knight in shining armor they first saw in their little girl and little boy dreams!

Virgo with Aquarius:

Both Virgo and Aquarius can be emotionally detached, so when they think they are headed for some kind of connection, they could end up in an intellectual discussion about what that means. If Virgo could ever get over being embarrassed and work up the courage to say what he or she would like to Shoot-the-Moon Aquarius, they may get past the detachment to something more physical. But alas, Virgo is all about actual hot-blooded sex and Aquarius just theorizes it.

Virgo with Pisces:

Put the Virgin together with the Fish and you have some of the most imaginative sex anyone's ever dreamed about. Pisces will do anything and everything, which appeals to Virgo's secret desires. Virgo wants pleasure and Pisces loves to please, so they both get what they want. But dreamy Pisces begins to irritate practical Virgo. And Virgo's "it's either black or white" analysis of the world sends Pisces into a panic. Soon they both wake up and realize it was all just a fantasy.

Virgo Celebrities And Dirty, Sexy, Funny

Jason Sudeikis:

Jason Sudeikis talked about his unorthodox weight loss plan in an interview for *Elle*[28]. He confirmed that an early walk on the treadmill isn't what helps him shed the pounds. No, he relies on the best workout partner he could have, his fiancée, Olivia Wilde. No need for a gym membership for this plan, all you need is lots of sex.

Health is a big priority for Virgo, so it is natural that Jason would work on his weight. Virgos also always have their eye on the prize; so working out with gorgeous Olivia will work twofold for Jason, weight loss and hot sex!

Jada Pinkett-Smith:

Jada Pinkett-Smith is prone to talking about her and husband. Will Smith's, sex life. In an interview with *Shape*[29] magazine, she got specific about some of the places they have had sex. One memorable time was in the limo on the way to the Academy Awards. Will was looking at her in a way that makes her wild. They never made it to the red carpet. And her makeup probably needed a bit of a touch up upon their arrival.

Jada, like all other Virgo women, seems to have a sixth sense for her man's sexual needs and will take care of them, whenever and wherever duty calls. Will's a lucky man!

Emmy Rossum:

When Emmy Rossum appeared on *Chelsea Lately*[30], she was asked the question everyone was dying to know: How does Emmy keep from accidentally being penetrated when filming those hot love scenes on *Shameless*? Emmy was only too happy to answer. Since the crew of *Shameless* wants realistic sex scenes without actually being real, they make Emmy wear a Vadge-Pad, something that resembles a triangular maxi-pad and acts as a buffer. And the guy wears a sock! That way they can lose themselves to the intensity of the scene without worrying that something's going to end up some place it's not supposed to be. She also said in an interview for *Cosmopolitan*[31] that guys confuse her with her *Shameless* character, Fiona, and think she's going to be the easy, have-sex on the-first-date kind of girl.

The Virgo woman's personality is two sided, the Vixen and the Virgin. They appear all sweet and innocent, but definitely have a more deviant side. In watching Emmy's character Fiona, people get to see both sides, but identify more with the Vixen than the sweet side, so it's easy to understand why people view Emmy in her real life from the sexy side.

Charlie Sheen:

Admitted sex addict, Charlie Sheen, stated that he doesn't pay for sex from prostitutes, but pays for them to leave. He mentioned in a *Playboy*[32] interview that he couldn't say he'd never be with one again. It's a hard call. He said part of it is soulless and part feels nourishing. And that it's like rolling the dice.

The Virgo man can have some kinky ideas about sex, so until he finds the right woman to settle down with, it may be easier to frequent a professional. Sounds as though Charlie is a creature of habit like other Virgo males, so he's right to never say never.

Virgo Celebrity List

August 23:
Kobe Bryant
Ant
Scott Caan
Rick Springfield
Jay Mohr
Layla Iskandar

August 24:
Rupert Grint
Vince McMahon
Dave Chappelle
Alex O'Loughlin
Cal Ripkin Jr.
Marlee Matlin
Steve Guttenberg
Carmine Giovinazzo
Mike Shanahan

August 25:
Billy Ray Cyrus
Blake Lively
Sean Connery
Tim Burton
Gene Simmons
Rachael Ray
Alexander Skarsgard
Rachael Bilson

Blair Underwood
Claudia Schiffer

August 26:
Macaulay Culkin
Chris Pine
Melissa McCarthy
John Mulaney
Kim Burrell

August 27:
Aaron Paul
Tom Ford
Chandra Wilson

August 28:
Jack Black
Shania Twain
Cassadee Pope
LeAnn Rimes
Armie Hammer
Daniel Stern
Jennifer Coolidge
David Fincher

August 29:
Lea Michele
William Levy

Carla Gugino
Elliott Gould
Temple Grandin

August 30:
Cameron Diaz
Warren Buffett
Michael Chiklis
Lisa Ling
Michael Michele

August 31:
Chris Tucker
Richard Gere
Sara Ramirez
Zack Ward

September 1:
Zendaya Coleman
Gloria Estefan
Barry Gibb
Rachael Zoe
Padma Lakshmi

September 2:
Mark Harmon
Salma Hayek
Keanu Reeves
Katt Williams
Terry Bradshaw
Camille Grammer

September 3:
Charlie Sheen
Shaun White
Nick Hall
DJ Envy

September 4:
Beyonce Knowles
Damon Wayans
Dr. Drew Pinsky
Khandi Alexander
Tom Watson
Adrienne Maloof

September 5:
Skandar Keynes
Rose McGowan
Michael Keaton
Werner Herzog
William Devane
Mavis Leno

September 6:
Idris Elba
Pippa Middleton
Rosie Perez
Jeff Foxworthy
Anika Nini Rose
Foxy Brown
Macy Gray
Swoosie Kurtz

September 7:
Evan Rachel Wood
Shannon Elizabeth
Devon Sawa
Michael Emerson
Tom Everett Scott

September 8:
Pink
Wiz Khalifa
Jonathan Taylor Thomas
Brooke Burke
David Arquette
Larenz Tate

September 9:
Adam Sandler
Hunter Hayes
Michael Buble
Hugh Grant
Michelle Williams
Eric Stonestreet

September 10:
Colin Firth
Misty Copeland
Ryan Phillippe
Karl Lagerfeld
Guy Ritchie
Randy Johnson
Coco Rocha

September 11:
Ludacris
Harry Connick Jr.
Taraji Henson
Moby
Virginia Madsen
Roxann Dawson

September 12:
Jennifer Hudson
Yao Ming
Emmy Rossum
Louis CK
Jennifer Nettles
James McCartney

September 13:
Ben Savage
Tyler Perry
Michelle Duggar
Fiona Apple
Stella McCartney

September 14:
Amy Winehouse
Sam Neill
Katie Lee
Bowser
Kimberly Williams Paisley

September 15:
Oliver Stone
Prince Harry
Dan Marino
Tommy Lee Jones
Lisa Vanderpump
Danny Nucci

September 16:
David Copperfield
Nick Jonas
Jennifer Tilley
Flor Ida
Marc Anthony
Amy Poehler
BB King
Mickey Rourke
Molly Shannon

September 17:
Phil Jackson
Joe Bastianich
Bebe Winans
Nate Berkus

September 18:
Jada Pinkett Smith
Patrick Schwarzenegger
James Marsden
Xzibit
Aisha Tyler

Jason Sudeikis
Holly Robinson Peete

September 19:
Jimmy Fallon
Alison Sweeny
Danielle Panabaker
Trisha Yearwood
Jeremy Irons
Mario Batali
Michael Symon

September 20:
Phillip Phillips
Sophia Loren
Aaron Paul
Asia Argento
Kristen Johnston
Moon Blooodgood

September 21:
Abby Lee Miller
Bill Murray
Stephen King
Alfonso Ribeiro
Faith Hill
Nicole Richie
Luke Wilson
Leonard Cohen
Ricki Lake

September 22:
Tom Felton
Joan Jett
Andrea Bocelli

LIBRA

September 23 – October 22

The Negotiator

September 23-October 22

Libra is the Renoir or Rembrandt of the zodiac when it comes to "painting" the scene for romantic and sexual rendezvous. Like a fine artist, they place every luxurious detail in a perfectly harmonious setting, from the lighting to the post coital finger food. Then they don ultra-sexy lingerie, turn on the music, and make sure that there's nice scented oil on the nightstand for sensuous massages.

Symbol: The Scales
Ruling Planet: Venus
Body Part Ruled: Kidneys
House Ruled: Seventh, the house of partnerships
Element: Air
Color: Blue, Pink
Stone: Opal
Key Phrase: I balance
Trait: Charm
Weakness: Indecisiveness
Quality: Cardinal

What Libra Is All About

Diplomatic is what I'm all about. I don't like conflict between myself and others, or between anyone for that matter. I do everything I can to avoid confrontations, to the point of telling people what I think they want to hear so we don't argue. I'll hide my true feelings just in case they don't agree with me. And I try to be the peacemaker when my friends are fighting with each other. I'm good at that, balancing things out and smoothing them over.

My symbol is the scales, which is how I'm able to keep things nice and even; but I have to be careful. Put too much on one side and the scales become unbalanced. That's kind of like my life. I have two extremes. On my own, my home is either, neat and beautifully decorated, or it's a mess until I can't stand it anymore.

On one hand, I'm independent, and on the other, I'm co-dependent. I can't explain it, with my intelligence you'd think I could just make up my mind and be one way or the other. But I have a hard time doing that. I'm indecisive. I go out to lunch with a friend, look at the menu, and just can't decide what to have. I'll wait until my friend orders, and end up saying, "I'll have what they're having." Sometimes I don't even like it, but I'll order it anyway.

Relationships are really important to me, not just the romantic ones, but all of them, family, business, friendships. I even have relationships with all the delivery people at work, the bank teller, and the butcher at the grocery store. It's always, "Hi Joe. How are the kids?" or "Good to see you, Sue. How was the vacation?" I like everyone and everyone likes me. But what's not to like?

I'm really sexy, maybe the sexiest in the zodiac. I'm charming and seductive, and can pretty much wrap whoever I want around my finger. But I'm willing to let you take the lead on what you want to do when it comes to sex. Don't get me wrong, there's plenty I like to do, but I'm not going to tell you off the bat. I don't want to hurt your feelings or embarrass you.

Later on, I'll tell you every little detail, so it can be perfect, like the greatest, hottest sex scene off the Silver Screen. I'll even help you set the scene with candles, scented oils, and lots of foreplay with that oil. It will be slow, sensual, and perfection.

I should warn you about a couple things. First, I expect you to be loyal, no fooling around on me. Second, I need this experience! If I don't get it from you, I'll find someone else to give it to me. And third, if you ask me about what I've been up to, I'll stand right there and look you in the baby blues, and deny everything. You know I don't want to hurt your feelings!

LIBRA WOMAN:

The Libra woman wants balance and symmetry in her life as well as in her relationships, including her many friendships. She likes to be enveloped with luxury and comfortable things, which is a big bonus for her love life. Or that should be, for her partner's love life, because he's the one who will benefit most from her being happy and contented. Some think the Libra woman is a diva, because she can seem slightly helpless. But it is the result of being indecisive and having trouble making up her mind. When she has a strong partner who takes care of the tough decisions for her, she seems much more confident. The secret is that she really is independent down deep, but prefers to be in a relationship. This is a woman who is in love with the idea of being in love!

She is the enchantress of the zodiac and is well schooled in the art of allure. Her charm is part of her seductive wiles. The important thing in relationships is the commitment for her, so part of her seduction technique is to get her man wrapped up in her, so he wants to be around. When that happens, she makes sure that everything is balanced and that they are equals, no dominates here, because she thinks responsibilities should be shared.

She is a big flirt, but it's pretty much meaningless and harmless. This seems contradictory because she likes to reel in her lovers, but there is a difference in innocent flirting and full on I'm-interested-in-making-you-mine mode. She appreciates her body and loves showing it off for you. So expect to see sexy scanty lingerie, or nothing at all, except maybe the sensuous oil dripping off her. When she feels completely comfortable, she'll act on all her fantasies, especially those involving a lot of mirrors and lights! Is she kinky? Everyone's idea of kink can be different, but yes, she is one of the more kinky women of zodiac. You'll love it!

LIBRA MAN:

The Libra man has a finely developed intuition and can realize when people have a hidden agenda; so don't think about trying to fool him. He is great at conversation and is well versed on many subjects, but especially the arts. Don't expect to babble about meaningless or trite topics; he's much more deep and will find it to be boring and so much drivel that you won't have another chance to make a better impression. Even though he is fair and reasonable, you need to brush up on current events or read some interesting books if you want to hold his attention.

This is a man who is willing to compromise because he believes in justice. Libra's sign is the Scales of Lady Justice, so it is natural for him to want to find resolutions to problems and to weigh both sides before making up his mind. But in his personal or sex life, this can create issues. If he doesn't have a partner or lover who helps him make decisions, he can spend too much time looking at all his options. This can lead to him sampling the wares of women he encounters, even though he has a committed relationship at home. Is he a big cheater? Possibly, but he will only really be invested in his love partner.

His main goal is to please his spouse or lover. But he needs to know exactly what she likes and what it will take for him to keep her satisfied and happy. He has studied the female body extensively, so he knows his way around all the sweet and tender parts. He also has a vivid imagination and will try just about anything to make sure she is brought to an orgasm each and every time. But it is so much easier if she tells him what gets her fired up, and what turns the sizzle into fizzle.

EROGENOUS ZONE:

The low back, from the waist to the buttocks, is the Libra hot zone. When a Libra says to pinch their cheeks, they don't mean the ones on their faces!

SEX POSITION:

Him, kneeling position with one leg forming "chair" for her to straddle!

SEX PROPS:

KY or any other sensuous jelly!

Who Gets Them Hot And Not So Much

Hottest Sex: Gemini, Leo, Sagittarius, Aquarius

One Night Stand (or Two): Aries, Taurus, Libra

Not So Much: Cancer, Virgo, Scorpio, Capricorn, Pisces

Libra with Aries:

In this case of opposite attraction, Libra and Aries make an instant love connection, for a few minutes! Initially, Aries fast-paced horizontal tango will get Libra going. And Libra's easy-going style will fuel Aries' fire. It may take more than one time to get it right, but by the third or fourth time, you will both be in ecstasy. Then it all starts going downhill. Libra likes every little thing to be passive and peaceful, while Aries loves a good argument just for the sake of squabbling. This is a case of men and women being from different planets and doesn't work very long.

Libra with Taurus:

Venus, the female half of the Divine Lovers, rules both Libra and Taurus, creating the love match of the Ages, right? Nope, think again. You'll tune in to each other sexually, and it will be great at least the first time, maybe more. But after you're basking in the rosy after-glow, problems start. Taurus likes relaxing at home, while Libra, the socializer, wants to go out and hang with friends. That may work once, but when the credit card bill comes in showing how much Libra spent treating guy and gal pals to drinks and noshes, frugal Taurus will close the card and the door to romance.

Libra with Gemini:

Gemini should bring along the latest sex manual when hooking up with Libra. These two will go through it backwards and forwards, and then start all over again. Sex is good? No, it's great, fantastic, and any other superlative you can think of! You both love talking about anything and everything. The only issue is that you also both can have a catty barb to your talkative tongues. Don't let it get the better of you. Keep your chats about all the things you have in common and that should take care of the problem. If both of you keep an eye on your finances, and Gemini can manage to only have eyes for Libra, this will be one great romance.

Libra with Cancer:

Sex between Libra and Cancer will be just about as intoxicating as a censored copy of the latest hot sexy novel! Take all the sex out, and what you have left is too boring to bother with. Cancer is way too reserved and sulky for Libra. And Cancer thinks the Libra charm is tawdry and shameful; but they are wrong of course, and could learn a thing or two in that department. It's better if these two just agree to disagree. They'll both end up disappointed if they attempt even one romp underneath the sheets!

Libra with Leo:

Leo loves to take charge in all areas of life, especially when it comes to sex. And Libra, whether they want to admit it, deep down wants someone to tell them what to do so they don't have to make the hard decisions. Libra is full of diplomacy, so will know exactly how to handle the Lion's delicate ego. If there are any disagreements or misunderstandings that Libra can't maneuver, they'll back off. Leo will then lavish them with love, gifts, flowers; and everything will be back to sweetness and light. This combo of beauty and charisma makes for the red-carpet couple of zodiac compatibility!

Libra with Virgo:

Virgo may seem a bit too much of a prude for the sensual Libra. But that's only because Libra hasn't a clue on how to turn Virgo on, and Virgo thinks the super affectionate Libra has an agenda of their own. Sex could be great, if they knew how to communicate with each other, and took time for foreplay, which they both love and need. Rather than doing what they both know how to do, they find fault with each other, and any chance for love or sex goes down the drain.

Libra with Libra:

Two people both ruled by Venus, Goddess of Love, should know how to please each other, right? Not so much, when they both think sex is a game. Sure it's the game of love, but when they're having so much fun, no one is taking the lead. So they may have great sex for a while, if they find a position where neither has to exert too much effort. But nothing will be happening on the relationship front. Relationships take a lot of work and with two people who can never make a decision, that isn't going to happen. They should just have their fun until they both find a better partner.

Libra with Scorpio:

Scorpio's fervor will grab Libra's interest right away, and the first several times will be amazing. They'll be at it for hours at a time with the Scorpion keeping Libra firmly wrapped in their arms. Libra will keep Scorpio tantalized, for a while at least. They need to have a good time while it lasts, because when it's over, it's over. Up close and personal, Scorpio will think Libra's playful ways are childish and will want a grown-up in their bed. Libra will think this is all too serious and will look to move on.

Libra with Sagittarius:

These two are both freedom loving, and highly spirited, when it comes to sexual adventures. Their sex will be exciting for both Libra and Sagittarius. They both like playing bedroom games, whether it's costumes and characters, spin the bottle, or something else that the two of them come up with on their own. The only issue to this being a permanent match will be if Libra can give Sagittarius a long lease, and deal with a rare affair or two. Of course, Libra can also play this game, when not getting what they need in their own bedroom. Open relationship? Hmm!

Libra with Capricorn:

Libra can initially be attracted to Capricorn's success and forcefulness. But once they head towards the bed, if they do at all, it will seem more boardroom than bedroom, which will be a total turn off for Libra. It'll be a snooze fest. That will just be the beginning of their problems. Capricorn believes in putting a little away, okay a LOT, for a rainy day. Libra thinks money was meant for spending, and you use an umbrella when it's raining. There's no middle ground for these two. They'll be lucky to make it as friends, but there's no chance at all as lovers.

Libra with Aquarius:

There's always talk about matches made in Heaven, but this one is made in the ethereal realm, where these two Air signs can soar unfettered by Earthly restraints. Anything that is unique or unusual will get them going. Not only are they great lovers, but also close friends, the kind that are life-long. They have so much in common when it comes to communication style; they both love talking, and their exchanges are easy, intelligent, and free flowing. And best of all, they'll both enjoy whispering sweet, or dirty nothings to each other!

Libra with Pisces:

The commonalities between Libra and Pisces are abundant, including nostalgia, romance, sentimentality, and affection. It seems like it would be the ultimate sexual dream team, but it ends up just being a short-lived fantasy. These two are so laid back, that neither takes the initiative to do more than a few smooches and a bit of fondling. Even though they may try for a few weeks, that will be that, and it will be over before it has really begun. Both need a more energetic demonstrative lover to get them started, and they just can't do it for each other!

Libra Celebrities And Dirty, Sexy, Funny

Gwyneth Paltrow:

On Howard Stern's *SiriusXM Radio Show*[33] Gwyneth shared a few sexual secrets. When he praised her for telling a friend of hers that the way to avoid fighting with her husband was to give him plenty of oral sex, she went on to say that couples don't have to fight: the woman just has to act like a girl and make her man feel like a man. And apparently the best way to do that is through of lots of blowjobs.

One thing that Libras are really into is pleasing their lovers. It sounds like Libra Gwyneth has it down to a T.

Bruno Mars:

In a *GQ*[34] interview, Bruno Mars talked about his feelings on getting down and dirty. He said that he enjoys singing about sex; it makes him feel sexy and is great for getting into a hot frame of mind. He also explained that his song, *Locked Out of Heaven*, is a tribute to the female body part that he likes the most. He has woven words of love and sex within many of his album tracks, which gets things going on.

As a Libra, it's appropriate that Bruno feels the way he does about this subject, because romantic music is a huge turn on for Libras, both male and female. Bruno has recorded some of the most passionate, romantic music around.

John Mayer:

In an interview with *Playboy*,[35] John Mayer elaborated on his relationship with ex, Jessica Simpson. He said that she was like a drug to him, like doing crack cocaine. He went on to say that if he'd been paying, he'd have a 10K habit and would sell everything he had just to keep it up.

Pretty serious statement, right? Well, that's what happens with the Libra addictive personality! Sex rehab?

Kim Kardashian:

E! Online[36] has the scoop on Kim Kardashian's interview and photo shoot for *Love Magazine*[37]. She shared things, maybe a tad too many things, about her sexual proclivities, stating that her favorite position is from behind. When asked if she were an animal what would she be, she said a seahorse so she could have sex with herself. She also said she loves being nude, which was made apparent by how much she reveals in her sexy clothes and in the featured full-frontal photo spread.

Nothing that Kim does should be seen as shocking! Libra women are known exhibitionists, so she's only doing what comes naturally.

Dakota Johnson:

In her interview for *Glamour*[38], Dakota Johnson talked about her role as the sexy Anastasia Steele in *50 Shades of Grey*. She said that she wanted to portray to the best of her ability the character's innocence, the attraction she felt for Christian Grey, and what she would do to be able to be with him. Some of her preparations involved being waxed more than any woman should ever have to be. She also said that the scenes in the Red Room were the most vulnerable, but also the most intimate and passionate. Being tied to the bed naked was powerful; there's something very freeing to turn over control to another person for even a few minutes.

Dakota was the perfect Anastasia! The way she tackled this role shows how a Libra can be submissive to their partner, when there is trust on both sides, and how they can take the sexual experience to new heights.

Libra Celebrity List

September 23:
Bruce Springsteen
Jason Alexander
Ray Charles
Julio Iglesias
Anthony Mackie
Elizabeth Pena

September 24:
Robert Irvine
Nia Verdalos
Ross Mathews

September 25:
Will Smith
Christopher Reeve
TI
Heather Locklear
Barbara Walters
Will Smith
Michael Douglas
Catherine Zeta-Jones
Michael Madsen
Scotties Pippen

September 26:
Christina Milian
Linda Hamilton
Serena Williams

Olivia Newton-John

September 27:
Lil Wayne
Meat Loaf
Gwyneth Paltrow
Avril Lavigne
Astro

September 28:
Hilary Duff
Naomi Watts
Dita Von Teese
Janeane Garofalo
Moon Zappa
Mira Sorvino

September 29:
Steven "Twitch" Boss
Bryant Gumbel
Erika Eleniak
Ian Mcshane
Jane Velez-Mitchell

September 30:
Monica Bellucci
Jenna Elfman
April Macie
Kieran Culkin

Fran Drescher
Marion Cotillard
Martin Hingis
Cissy Houston

October 1:
Julie Andrews
Randy Quaid
Zach Galifianakis
Mark McGwire
Jimmy Carter

October 2:
Kelly Ripa
Donna Karan
Brianna Brown
Sting
Lorraine Bracco

October 3:
Gwen Stefani
Neve Campbell
Ashlee Simpson
Seann William Scott
Clive Owen
India Arie
Lindsey Buckingham

October 4:
Russell Simmons
Anne Rice

Dakota Johnson
Alicia Silverstone
Susan Sarandon
Christoph Waltz
Rachel Leigh Cook
Live Schreiber

October 5:
Grant Hill
Guy Pearce
Nicky Hilton
Kate Winslet
Parminder Nagra
Daniel Baldwin

October 6:
Jourdan Miller
Elisabeth Shue
Jeremy Sisto

October 7:
Simon Cowell
John Cougar Mellencamp
Toni Braxton
Yo Yo Ma
Joy Behar
Jayne Torvill

October 8:
Bruno Mars
Sigourney Weaver

Nick Cannon
Matt Damon
Cece Winans

October 9:
Scotty McCready
Scott Bakula
Sharon Osbourne

October 10:
David Lee Roth
Mya
Mario Lopez
Bai Ling
Brett Favre
Nora Roberts

October 11:
Matt Bomer
Luke Perry
Michelle Trachtenberg
Steve Young
Stephen Moyer
Joan Cusack
Michelle Wie

October 12:
Hugh Jackman
Kirk Cameron
Marion Jones

Bode Miller
Michael Wolfe

October 13:
Jerry Rice
Sammy Hagar
Ashanti
Nancy Kerrigan
Sacha Baron Cohen
Marie Osmond
Billy Bush
Paul Simon
Kelly Preston
Beverly Johnson

October 14:
Jay Pharoah
Ralph Lauren
Jon Seda
Harry Anderson
Usher

October 15:
Tito Jackson
Sarah Ferguson
Penny Marshall
Emeril Lagasse
Vanessa Marcil

October 16:
Flea

John Mayer
Suzanne Somers
Tim Robbins
Kim Wayans

October 17:
Eminem
Margot Kidder
Alan Jackson
Wyclef Jean
Felicity Jones
George Wendt
Ernie Els
Chris Lowell

October 18:
Zac Efron
Martina Navratilova
Ne-Yo
Jean-Claude Van Damme
Lindsey Vonn
Mike Ditka
Pam Dawber
Chuck Lorre
Wynton Marsalis

October 19:
Michael Gambon
Evander Holyfield
Floyd Mayweather

John Lithgow
Chris Kattan

October 20:
Candice Swanepoel
Viggo Mortensen
Tom Petty
Danny Boyle
Snoop Dogg

October 21:
Kim Kardashian
Ariana Rodriguez
Ken Watanabe
Amber Rose
Carrie Fisher
Jade Jagger

October 22:
Shaggy
Jesse Tyler Ferguson
Jeff Goldblum
Christopher Lloyd
Jonathan Lipnicki
Shelby Lynne
Deepak Chopra
Spike Jonze
Saffron Burrows
Brian Boitano

SCORPIO

October 23 – November 21

The Lover

October 23-November 21

Scorpio is the most erotic sign of the zodiac! Their magnetism and prowess can't be ignored or denied. They never waste time on frivolity as sex isn't a game to these sexy creatures; it is serious stuff and they are masters at it. They also love their toys, sex toys that is, to enhance the act. Look for a full drawer in the nightstand!

Symbol: Scorpion, Eagle, Snake, and the mythical Phoenix
Ruling Planet: Pluto
Body Part Ruled: Reproductive organs
House Ruled: Eighth, the house of birth, death, regeneration, and sex
Element: Water
Color: Scarlet
Stone: Topaz
Key Phrase: I desire
Trait: Idealism
Weakness: Jealousy
Quality: Fixed

What Scorpio Is All About

I don't know what it is, but some people act like they are scared to death of me. Maybe it's my intensity, or the way I can see right through them and know what they're thinking. I guess maybe I'd be scared too, if I weren't me. But I'd rather be me, someone who knows exactly what I want, instead of someone wandering through life without a clue.

I wake up each morning knowing what I'm going to do and ready to go for the brass ring. There's no standing on the sidelines waiting for something to come my way. I'm out there making things happen. I'm independent, almost to a fault, but I can accomplish absolutely anything I set my mind to, no matter how huge or small. I like being in control of my destiny. I can be extreme, but if you're not willing to do what it takes to get what you want, how are you ever going to get it?

Some people think I'm possessive or jealous. But that's not it at all. It's about protection. Who wouldn't want to protect those they love, especially the *one* they love? I am so loyal to those who stand by me. I would walk through fire for them. If someone isn't loyal or betrays me, I may want to throw them in the fire!

I have a great memory and will always remember even the smallest kindness that someone does for me. Those things will gain my respect and trust, as long as I know they are sincere, with no strings attached. No manipulation for me; I don't like ulterior motives.

I'm at my best when I'm in control. When I'm not, I can feel threatened, and it can be scary for me. I feel safe when I have the all the power. That's how I'm able to fuel my success, because no one knows what really makes me tick.

For me, sex is the total physical and emotional package. I want to feel the intensity and the passion of making love to my equal. I have awesome vitality and can go all night long, over and over. So, I have to have someone who can keep up with me. Fantasies and role-playing are big turn-ons for me, since I can be or do anything that I like. I guess I'm an actor or actress at heart. Time for my close up, Mr. DeMille!

Don't suggest fantasies to me if you don't plan on following through, because I will definitely hold you to them. Then if you back out, I won't be a happy camper. Of course I can compromise, but I say what I mean and mean what I say, and expect the same from you. Especially about something so exciting! If I tell you I'm going to rock your world, you'd better believe it's going to happen.

Seduction is an art that I have mastered. And don't think I'm just bragging, because I'm not. I don't do that. I'm just stating a fact. Sure it takes practice, but practice makes perfect. I know how to please you perfectly. And I won't be shy about telling you how to please me. Don't worry, I won't make you ask, I'll let you know. In fact, I'll be your guide!

SCORPIO WOMAN:

The Scorpio woman is intense, but she can also put forth a slightly shy, cool demeanor that might fool you into thinking she's a push over. That's until you look her squarely in the eyes! It doesn't matter what color they are, when a pair of Scorpio peepers stare you down, you will know it. And it's then that you'll know the meaning of intensity. But don't let that scare you away. With a Scorpio woman, intensity relates to passion; she is the most passionate woman of the zodiac. She likes to be in charge of every aspect of her life. If you're a man who is all machismo and doesn't let your woman have the final word, at least part of the time, either get over yourself or you'll have to let this one get away. You'll wish you hadn't!

Scorpio is an independent woman, and can take care of herself completely, thank you very much! This doesn't mean she wants to be alone, or likes it, but she doesn't jump into anything lightly. She may not let you know it up front, but she loves relationships that are committed. Once she can trust you enough to even consider giving you her heart, she'll let you know everything you need to know on the subject. But don't push her; it needs to be on her terms. Sex is serious business for the Lady Scorpion and she needs someone who feels the same way. She's got a great sense of humor and can laugh it up with the best of them, but not in the bedroom. If you want someone who will joke and poke fun about what happens in bed, you should go for a Sagittarius but never a Scorpio.

She doesn't have any tolerance for a man who isn't her sexual match. It doesn't mean she thinks she's all that.

She just has her own standards and needs someone who can keep her pace. She just doesn't want to have to drag you along. If you can keep up, she will make sure you are well satisfied. You'd be a fool to let this one get away!

SCORPIO MAN:

Unusual is usually a word reserved for Aquarius, but it also applies to the Scorpio man. He is different from all the other men of the zodiac. Why should this be? Although he has the rep as being a hound dog, he's actually into commitment just like the female Scorpio. And like his counterpart, he won't let you know right away.

The Scorpio man has a magnetism and charisma about him that can't be denied. And he doesn't even have to work at it. It just comes naturally. And then he has his unusual ticks, like his reaction to scent; he loves smelling his sexual partner. Of course, that means that she's going to smell good, because he's into the perfection of the female body, and B. O. doesn't fall in that category.

Like the Lady Scorp, he has the same intense eyes that can burn into your very being, or at least burn through your clothes. It's as if he can already see what lies beneath, before even underdressing you. Maybe that's where the phrase "undressing with your eyes" comes from. But he also has the ability to sense who you are as a person, what your motives are, if you have any, and whether you can be trusted.

He is a sexual master and will learn anything and everything he can to please you. Love, as well as sex, are serious subjects for him; no games, just getting down to business, the business of seduction and satisfaction. The only playing he does is when he plays for keeps. He has exceptional staying power. Whether he is still on the hunt for a suitable partner, or is going at it for days on end, he'll never lose steam. So be prepared, if you think you're up to it, and go for it! You won't be disappointed!

EROGENOUS ZONE:

Other signs may think the genital area is their erogenous zone, but only Scorpio has the right to this claim.

SEX POSITION:

Any, as long they get to be the boss. But, if they have to pick just one, it will always be the infamous "69"! Scorpios have no fear of the dark, so blindfolds can satisfy a major fetish.

SEX PROPS:

It's got to be Ben Wah Balls for the ladies and riding crops for the guys.

Who Gets Them Hot And Not So Much

Hottest Sex: Cancer, Virgo, Capricorn, Pisces

One Night Stand (or Two): Aries, Taurus, Scorpio, Sagittarius, Aquarius

Not So Much: Gemini, Leo, Libra

Scorpio with Aries:

Both Scorpio and Aries thrive on the power play, so they can expect to have seriously hot sex while playing one-upmanship. They will challenge each other to do things more and more outrageous. They will be walking around grinning ear to ear, if they can even walk at all. These two can have jealous streaks and really go at it, but the make-up sex is so wild, you'd think they fight just so they can make up. Their spats can turn in to sparring matches, complete with the boxing gloves. So unless they plan on never getting out of bed, they need to move on to someone that may be tamer in the bedroom, but will be less volatile out of it.

Scorpio with Taurus:

Taurus will stand toe to toe with Scorpio, match every sexual move he or she makes, and possibly come up with a few they've never heard of before. The sex between them is amazing. Scorpio keeps Taurus in awe, and Taurus is always ready to do whatever it takes to please Scorpio. If only they weren't both such hard heads, they might be able to turn this into a committed deal instead of a frolic. But there's not much chance of that, because both dig their heels in, and are unwilling to compromise. So this combo ends up having a pretty short shelf life.

Scorpio with Gemini:

Gemini's raunchy words will get Scorpio so aroused that the two of them will go at it for hours, never even coming up for air. Gemini will use their brilliant mind to find novel positions, and Scorpio will instantly act on them. They'll have a great time simply talking with one another because they are so fascinated by their differences. But after a while, the same things they're initially thrilled by will be the same ones that spell the end. Scorpio will find Gemini to be childish and irresponsible, and Gemini will think all that Scorp intensity is way too much to handle. So they need to enjoy it while it lasts and take their differences elsewhere.

Scorpio with Cancer:

Cancer is a scorching match for Scorpio. While not as kinky or adventurous as Scorpio, Cancer is willing to learn. They may feign embarrassment at some of the Scorpion's demands in the bed or elsewhere, but they'll secretly be raring to give anything and everything a try. Cancer is more tranquil than Scorpio on the surface, but can be clingy and a bit angst ridden underneath. However, these traits actually excite Scorpio. The best relationships are full of give and take. The Scorpion and the Crab fit the bill for success as lovers and life partners.

Scorpio with Leo:

A match like this could be hellacious for other signs, but not these two. Sure they have their differences, but who doesn't? Leo can think he or she is the cat's meow in the sack, and Scorpio can go so far as to think Leo's just a sack of shit, but that only lasts half a minute. Two big personalities like these are bound to clash once in a while. Leo demands to be the center of attention everywhere, and becomes pouty when he or she is feeling slighted. Scorpio knows how to rule in the bedroom, but is willing to let Leo be the King or Queen of the domain. Any squabbles that happen only make for scorching hot sex later on!

Scorpio with Virgo:

Virgo's shy initial response to Scorpio's straightforward approach to sex will intrigue the Scorpion to no end. Deep inside, Virgo will be driven crazy by what they perceive to be their supreme sexual partner, and they won't be wrong. Scorpio will have Virgo all aflutter, like a virginal schoolboy or girl, which just happens to be a roleplaying fantasy for this seemingly innocent one. When Scorpio has made Virgo feel safe, all their secret desires will be revealed, and fulfilled, for a lifetime.

Scorpio with Libra:

Sex between these two won't even make for a good one-night stand. Sure, they'll still make the attempt, as Libra will initially find Scorpio's wildness exciting, and Scorpio will succumb to Libra's charm; but this is only going to last for a heartbeat. Libra's approach to sex is all about shits and giggles, while Scorpio takes sex as seriously as nourishing their bodies. In fact, it is their nourishment. This is definitely one to avoid, so neither is left disappointed.

Scorpio with Scorpio:

The first few times will have you going at it like rabbits. But then one rabbit will wind up in a pot on the stove. Think *Fatal Attraction*! It's not worth the bunny sacrifice no matter how scalding the sex is. A relationship between two Scorpions can stir up so much jealousy that they sting each other to death. So, when looking at another Water sign for a permanent bed and life partner, definitely opt for Cancer or Pisces.

Scorpio with Sagittarius:

These two can rub each other the wrong way, so much so, that even if they started out as friends, that will soon go kaput with any attempt at an affair. Scorpio will start out being fascinated with Sagittarius' mind and gregariousness, and Scorpio's ardent approach to life and sex will grab the interest of Sagittarius. As fast as the freshness wears off, sex will begin to smell like something rotten. Scorpio will think Sag is somewhat coocoo and flighty, while Sagittarius will think the Scorpion is too hotheaded. Better for them to keep the friendship and skip the sex.

Scorpio with Capricorn:

Put together two of the most serious signs of the zodiac and you'll have some super-serious sexuality going, and everything else that a lasting relationship requires. Scorpio will strip away the prudish façade that Capricorn pretends to hide behind, and Capricorn will gladly unleash their sexual hunger. They'll end up having long, slow, sex sessions that last for days. Scorpio gets to dominate, and Capricorn gets to cut loose. This is one for the long term, and both will get exactly what they want.

Scorpio with Aquarius:

Bizarre could be the key word for these two coming together, if they ever get close to that. Aquarius has their head in the clouds, while Scorpio's idea of head is something entirely different. Scorpio just wants to get down to it, while Aquarius would rather philosophize or talk about it. It's also hard to keep the Scorpion primed when Aquarius goes on about children starving in India or some other global problem. Scorpio is one of the most compassionate signs of the zodiac, but there's a time and place for certain conversations. And when Scorpio is ready to ravage, that is not the time! This combo is just too peculiar to endure.

Scorpio with Pisces:

Both of these signs are intuitive and can read each other's minds and desires without ever communicating in words. Scorpio is more take charge, and Pisces is more passive, which makes for the perfect combination. The Scorpion can be the protector, and the Fish will come alive when he or she feels secure. With their vivid imaginations, their sexual fantasies may take on a life of their own. But they both will be right there in body and soul to live every single one!

Scorpio Celebrities And Dirty, Sexy, Funny

Katy Perry:

In an interview with *Chelsea Handler*[39], Katy Perry said that the longest time she'd gone without sex was six months, maybe a year tops. She also said that she carries around rose quartz to attract men, but added that maybe she should tone it down with some amethyst. Ultimately, the most important thing to her is the connection. She's not really strict, but doesn't do the one-night stand bit. She laid it all out with *WiLD 94.9's Nessa*[40], when she was asked if she was finally going to release some music with her BFF Rihanna. She said no, but they would have sex, jokingly, after pleading the fifth on several questions about positions and dirty sex. She went on to answer hump or dump questions, saying she'd hump Drake and dump Chris Brown!

Katy fits the bill as a red-blooded Scorpio. First of all, Scorpio's rarely go for long periods of time without sex.

Second, most have a spiritual belief like Katy's energy stones. And finally, Scorpio's are very sexual, but usually go for more than a one-night stand.

Leonardo DiCaprio:

Heartthrob Leonardo DiCaprio has dated a bevy of beauties over the last few years, including Bar Refaeli, Erin Heatherton, Blake Lively, Gisele Bundchen, Toni Garrn, and Nina Agdai. But when Gayle King interviewed him on *CBS This Morning*[41], Leo said that supermodel beauty isn't what he finds most attractive in a woman. He stressed that a sense of humor, humility, and no drama is what he's really looking for. This may be a bit hard to believe, especially since his reputation precedes him, as one of the great playboys of Hollywood. Seems like some of his sexy exploits in the *Wolf of Wall Street* could be closer to his true sexual nature.

Scorpio can be a man or woman of extremes, which clearly describes Leo. He dates all those beauties, but wants a drama-free life. Not to say that drama follows beautiful woman around, but when you add fame into the mix, some things are going to go down.

Gerard Butler:

On *Howard Stern SiriusXM*[42], Gerard Butler 'fessed up to having sex with Brandi Glanville even though at the time he only knew her as Brandi, no last name. Brandi had previously shared with Andy Cohen on *Watch What*

Happens Live that Gerard was the most famous man she'd ever had sex with, and gave him an eleven on the scale of one to ten. Gerard told Howard that he and Brandi had hung out at a beach party, and one thing led to another. He went on to say that he was less than happy that she blabbed because some things are supposed to be kept private.

Gerard is the perfect example of a true Scorpio. Until they've made a commitment, Scorpios may have the occasional one-night stand, but they want their sex lives to be kept out of the spotlight.

Ryan Gosling:

In an interview for *Slate.com*[43], Ryan Gosling discussed his chemistry with Eve Mendes in *The Place Beyond the Pines*. He said that he likes to think their chemistry comes directly from them, but thinks the real credit goes to director, Derek Clanfrance, who worked on drawing it out of them. When asked if men are as nervous as women in sex scenes, Ryan replied that most of the responsibility for how the two interact falls on the man, and that he felt Eva was vulnerable, it was his duty to make sure to block her in some of the nude scenes. He also told the *Huffington Post*[44] that sex between him and Michelle Williams in *Blue Valentine* felt very real because it was authentic. So much so that there was a battle to get the rating changed from NC-17 to R!

Scorpios exude sensuousness and sexuality so it is no wonder that the rating could be an issue when they're on the screen. Ryan also shows the compassionate side of Scorpio in his comments about feeling protective of Eva Mendes. True to Scorpio, he's both sensitive and in control!

Scorpio Celebrity List

October 23:
Michael Crichton
Nancy Grace
Pele
Dwight Yoakam
Ryan Reynolds
Weird Al Yankovic
Barron Hilton
Ang Lee

October 24:
Kevin Kline
PewDiePie
Monica
Drake
Adrienne Bailon

October 25:
Katy Perry
Tracy Nelson
Ciara
Pablo Picasso

October 26:
Hillary Rodham Clinton
Keith Urban
Cary Elwes

Jaclyn Smith
Pat Sajak

October 27:
Ruby Dee
Lee Greenwood
John Cleese

October 28:
Julie Roberts
Bill Gates
Brad Paisley
Joaquin Phoenix
Frank Ocean
Auguste Escoffier

October 29:
Kate Jackson
Gabrielle Union
Winona Ryder
Ben Foster

October 30:
Ivanka Trump
Harry Hamlin
Gavin Rossdale

October 31:
Dan Rather
Willow Smith
Piper Perabo
John Candy
Rob Schneider

November 1:
Jenny McCarthy
Larry Flint
Lyle Lovett

November 2:
k. d. Lang
Nelly
David Schwimmer

November 3:
Roseanne
Kendall Jenner
Dolph Lungren
Kate Capshaw
Dolph Lundgren
Charles Bronson
Anna Wintour

November 4:
Sean Puffy Combs
Matthew McConaughey
Ralph Macchio

Curtis Stone
Walter Cronkite

November 5:
Ike Turner
Famke Janssen
Vivian Leigh
Art Garfunkel
Tilda Swinton
Bryan Adams
Tatum O'Neal

November 6:
Thandie Newton
Sally Fields
Emma Stone
Ethan Hawke
Rebecca Romijn
Mike Nichols
Maria Shriver

November 7:
Billy Graham
Bethany Mota
Lorde
Jason London
Jeremy London
Marie Curie
Joni Mitchell

November 8:
Bonnie Raitt
Parker Posey
Tara Reid
Gordon Ramsay

November 9:
Lou Ferrigno

November 10:
Sinbad
MacKenzie Phillips
Miranda Lambert
Roy Scheider
Brittany Murphy
Martin Luther
Richard Burton
Ellen Pompeo

November 11:
Demi Moore
Leonardo DiCaprio
Calista Flockhart
Stanley Tucci

November 12:
David Schwimmer
Ryan Gosling
Tanya Harding
Grace Kelly
Anne Hathaway

Sammy Sosa
Neil Young

November 13:
Whoopi Goldberg
Gerard Butler
Jimmy Kimmel
Steve Zahn
Garry Marshall

November 14:
Claude Monet
Prince Charles
Josh Duhamel
Travis Barker

November 15:
Sam Waterston
Shailene Woodley
Georgia O'Keeffe
Jimmy Choo
Roberto Cavalli

November 16:
Lisa Bonet
Maggie Gyllenhaal
Oksana Baiul

November 17:
Martin Scorsese
Rachel McAdams

Lauren Hutton
Lorde
Rock Hudson
RuPaul
Danny DeVito

Troy Aikman
Jena Malone
Michael Strahan
Ken Griffey Jr.

November 18:
Linda Evans
Owen Wilson
David Ortiz

November 19:
Larry King
Jodie Foster
Meg Ryan
Ted Turner
Rocco DiSpirito
Tyga
Calvin Klein

November 20:
Veronica Hamel
Michael Clifford
Future
Bo Derek

November 21:
Goldie Hawn
Marlo Thomas
Colleen Ballinger
Carley Rae Jepsen

SAGITTARIUS

November 22 – December 21

The Traveler

November 22-December 21

Sagittarius has their seductive powers down. The Archer hones and perfects their skills until they can call themselves masters, beating out most other signs, or at least ranking with the best. They have been known to render their lovers helpless to their advances. Hello Don Juan!

Symbol: The Archer
Ruling Planet: Jupiter
Body Part Ruled: Liver
House Ruled: Ninth, the house of religion, knowledge, higher education and travel
Element: Fire
Color: Purple
Stone: Turquoise
Key Phrase: I see
Trait: Optimism
Weakness: Undiplomatic
Quality: Mutable

What Sagittarius Is All About

If the *Travel Channel* posted one person's picture, it would be a picture of me. I am the ultimate traveler. You know that saying, "The world is my oyster"? It was written about me. Well, if it wasn't, it should have been! Everything is a great adventure to me, even going to the grocery store. I don't just zip in, grab my stuff, and go. No, I go aisle by aisle to find the most exotic produce, spices, condiments, and other things from around the world.

Then, I think about all the countries where my purchases came from, and make a list of all the ones I've been to. In my head, I'm already planning my next big trip. Every time, I plan to go somewhere new, but there are just some I've been to over and over again because I love them so much. I have a huge bucket list of where I'm planning to go, and cross them off one by one. Taj Mahal. Check. Bora Bora. Check.

Some of my trips have been exciting, daring, and downright dangerous. But that's okay, it gets my adrenaline going, and I don't have to ask for anyone's approval. I'm so independent; I just throw what I think I'll need in a backpack and take off. If I forget anything, I can usually go without, or find something in a little bazaar.

When the mood strikes me, and it often does, I go on a spiritual journey to an ashram in India or a sacred place in the Far East. It makes me feel so connected to the universe and all of creation. I look forward to learning something no matter where I go. In fact, I *have* to learn something; the world is my university as well as my oyster.

Of course, I have a bit of a wandering eye, so no matter where I am, I'm always checking out the locals to see if I can find someone worth my interest. Hey, I said that I have to learn something on my travels and what better way to test my new knowledge than by trying out the new skills that go with it.

I'm not held back by any emotional hang-ups, so I can go off exploring both the countries and the people. Some may be upset by my inability to make commitments easily, but I usually don't stay around in one place long enough to commit anyway. Let's just say that I'm an expert at the one-night stand. But you'll always know what you're getting up front!

Now, don't get me wrong! This doesn't mean that if I find the right person, I can't be with them for the long run. I just need to have a really, really, long leash, so that I don't have to sacrifice my freedom. And I need someone who can keep up with me, so boredom doesn't set in. If that happens, I have a tough time. Just don't let me get bored!

SAGITTARIUS WOMAN:

The Sagittarius woman is a creature with many dimensions and layers. She loves adventures and taking risks, just like her male counterpart. She doesn't like advice from other people and would rather rely on her own instincts. This can be an issue if she isn't as in touch with her intuition as she thinks she is.

She is a fascinating woman, who has difficulty staying interested, but not as much as the Sag man. She is adventurous and will want to roam the world with the best of them. She is quite capable of going it alone, but thinks it would be so much more fun to have you come along. She's less inclined to need that extra-long leash, like the male of her species. Her big thing is boredom. If you let her get bored, she will be gone to find someone who is more exciting to her. She loves having a good time, so if you play your cards right, you'll be able to keep her interested with lots of games, not game playing, but actual games like hide and seek or tag.

Of course, there have to be rewards attached to winning the game. If not, and you hide first, she may just not come find you. But use the game as a prelude to sex, with the winner choosing all the details, where, how, and how long, and she will find you before you have even settled into your hiding position. Speaking of positions, this Sag is well versed on the subject, but always ready to try something new. She is definitely capable of the happily ever after once she finds the right guy. If you want it to be you, make sure to keep her stimulated, and she'll be yours for a lifetime. Most likely!

SAGITTARIUS MAN:

It may be a challenge to get a good feel for the Sagittarius man. The chase is what he's all about, so while you think you're chasing him, he could be chasing some other woman, or even two at the same time. If Sagittarius tells you that he's into you, he is. The fact is that he can be into someone else too. He's an optimist when it comes to romance and thinks every woman may be the one! And he has a huge problem with commitment. His idea of the perfect situation would be a woman who is open minded about his escapades.

Sagittarius has a great sense of humor, and the two of you can spend a lot of time laughing and having great fun both in the bed and out. He loves adventures, which can be anything from bungee jumping to canoeing down the Amazon. If you want to have a chance with him at all, you need to be just as adventurous as he is. In fact, to really grab his interest, book a surprise trip for an African safari or trekking the Great Wall of China. But if you want to make sure he comes back to you, you'd better book this as a trip for two, and be prepared to do all the stuff he does, whether it's swimming in shark infested waters, or eating fried crickets.

He's spontaneous, and isn't afraid to take risks. So having sex in public places, where he could possibly get caught, won't faze him in the least. If you think this is the man of your dreams, you have to be willing to go through a nightmare or two, be open to things that are wild and crazy, be ready to do things you never thought you'd do before, and most importantly, enjoy yourself in the process. It won't be that bad. If you have your sights set on a Sagittarius man, you probably already have it in you to do it all anyway. When the Sagittarius man finally finds the right person, he will accept a shorter leash, within reason, and be committed 110%.

EROGENOUS ZONE: The hips and thighs. Strokes to both areas are what do it for Sagittarius, especially along the inner thighs.

SEX POSITION:

The Saddle! She gets to hold on to his thighs and he gets to caress hers! Board games of the sexual nature make the top of their fetish list.

SEX PROPS:

Leave a hand written note describing a sexual fantasy on Sagittarius' pillow and you will get big results.

Who Gets Them Hot And Not So Much

Hottest Sex: Aries, Gemini, Leo, Libra, Aquarius
One Night Stand (or Two): Scorpio, Sagittarius
Not So Much: Taurus, Cancer, Virgo, Capricorn, Pisces

Sagittarius with Aries:

When there's fire there's fire, and these two Fire signs are hot enough to burn any building down. Aries loves to take the initiative and will get Sagittarius to agree to any room in the house. Sagittarius has a penchant for the great outdoors and will take Aries on an adventure of sexual romps around the globe. The problem is that there will be a lot of spats and jockeying for power. Of course, there will be just as much making up, which may be even hotter. These two have enough passion to go the distance, even if they bicker all the way.

Sagittarius with Taurus:

There's nothing good that can come from this pairing. Sagittarius is a prankster and is apt to pull something in the bed that will irritate Taurus, since he or she considers their bedroom to be the sanctuary of the house. Taurus wants to take charge, and Sagittarius wants lots of freedom. The Bull likes to stash away lots of money, and the Archer thinks cash is for spending. These two have nothing in common and will be on each other's nerves in a flash. This is a better walk-on-by situation.

Sagittarius with Gemini:

These two are opposites by sign only. In all other aspects, they are peas in a pod. Gemini loves talking dirty, and Sagittarius is delighted to participate, or listen intently. There aren't many things that these two aren't up for, things that would make a lot of other signs blush. One thing is for sure; they will never be bored together. The issue is that neither of these freedom-loving signs can take the other seriously when it comes to anything more than a few nights or days of good sex. They both have commitment phobia, so unfortunately the relationship will go nowhere.

Sagittarius with Cancer:

When Sagittarius and Cancer get together, the first time or two will make both of them very happy. The Archer can break the Crab out of their shell with naughty moves. There will be no need to communicate in words because the bodies will be doing all the talking. But then reality sets in. Cancer is a big homebody, and Sagittarius thinks their home is the world, and they need to visit it often. This will make Cancer resentful, but not as much as when Sagittarius follows his or her wandering eye into some other bedroom. That's when it's really a deal-breaker!

Sagittarius with Leo:

This is another hot Fire sign combo. Both Sagittarius and Leo know exactly what they love doing and neither is afraid to ask for it. The sex is more than great; it's fantastic. They will probably need a sound proofed room when they really get going. This is a pair that loves to have a good time, and will play host to all their friends. But it is also a good long-term relationship in the making.

Sagittarius with Virgo:

If Sagittarius and Virgo are friends, they need to make no attempts at taking it to the next level; the elevator simply doesn't go there, or will break down on the way. While they may get along as buddies, in a relationship, Sagittarius will think Virgo is a prudish bore and Virgo won't trust Sag for an instant. This one's never going to happen!

Sagittarius with Libra:

Fun loving Sagittarius will adore Libra's easygoing attitude, and find it refreshing. Libra will find Sagittarius' casual sexual approach very exciting. Together they will come up with more positions than most all other sign combinations. On top of that, they will have lots of fun! Libra may prove to be the one sign that can keep Sagittarius on the straight and narrow with their love of life and laid back style. Sagittarius will be so enamored that they won't be inclined to wander away from this one.

Sagittarius with Scorpio:

This match is a no-go from the get-go. Sagittarius and Scorpio have trouble being friends, let alone lovers. Scorpio demands loyalty and non-stop attention from their partner. Sagittarius won't listen to demands from anyone. Scorpio wants to be in charge, both in the bedroom and all other areas of the relationship. Sagittarius will be saying "What relationship?" and be off to roam the world before Scorpio knows they're gone. They should both just run in the opposite direction at the start.

Sagittarius with Sagittarius:

Another fiery hot combo of two Fire signs, the sex between Sag and Sag may be even better than between Sag and Leo or Sag and Aries. These two are up for anything, absolutely anything. When the urge strikes, they'll be outta their clothes quicker than you can blink your eyes. And it can happen anywhere, anytime, as they have no fear or shame about being caught. But when they walk out of the bedroom, the woods, or wherever else they have been going at it, things will take a turn. Neither will want to be tied down to the other, so they're best as casual sex buddies, nothing more. They'll have to look elsewhere to find someone to keep them interested for the long haul.

Sagittarius with Capricorn:

Sagittarius and Capricorn are as different as day and night. Sagittarius' little ray of sunshine optimism will make Capricorn want to puke, while Sag will think the Goat is the most boring thing around. Sagittarius spends money like there's no tomorrow, while Capricorn stashes it away like the next big depression is upon us. So what's the chance these two will make it to the bedroom? Slim to none. The Archer should go hunting elsewhere, while the Goat moves on to greener pastures.

Sagittarius with Aquarius:

Sagittarius' philosophical views can intrigue Aquarius, while Sagittarius will be fascinated with Aquarius' futuristic ideas. At first, their bedroom antics may not quite mesh due to their different ways of thinking. But just wait until they have a few practice sessions out of the way! Aquarius doesn't mind that Sagittarius requires a long, long leash and will give it to them. The Sagittarius quick wit and verbal repartee will seem like intellectual foreplay for Aquarius. Before hitting the sheets, these two might as well send out the wedding announcements!

Sagittarius with Pisces:

Sexual attraction will be electric between Sagittarius and Pisces from the first time their eyes meet. Sag will introduce Pisces to a plethora of exciting things they never knew existed. Pisces is more than willing to try it all, and with their vivid imagination, they might be able to teach Sagittarius a trick or two. But away from the bedroom, Sagittarius will start to get restless. Pisces needs faithful and that sure as hell isn't Sagittarius in this combo. The longer they stay together, the unhappier Pisces will be and the more Sagittarius will be chomping at the bit to get away.

Sagittarius Celebrities And Dirty, Sexy, Funny

Brad Pitt:

In a *Bustle* [45]interview, Brad Pitt said that he and Angelina Jolie have a great place to have sex right at home, in the grotto behind the pool's waterfall. He also shared that Angelina still has all her bad girl moves, and that all their bedroom, or grotto, antics are too hot for public eyes.

Sagittarius is always up for a big adventure in sex as well as in life, so it is only natural that Brad would be looking for places and positions that would satisfy this part of his psyche.

Scarlett Johansson:

In a *contactmusic.com*[46] interview, Scarlett Johansson revealed that when she's feeling extra raunchy, or wants to be a little crazy, she likes having sex in the backseat of the car. She told *Daily Mail UK*[47] that she has never been promiscuous, but did admit to getting an HIV test every six months when she was single. Because of being voted Esquire Magazine's Sexiest Woman Alive, not once, but twice, people get the wrong idea about her. She told Barbara Walters, when making Barbara's *Most Fascinating People*[48] List that she thinks it's liberating to film such realistic love scenes in her movies.

Sagittarians love having encounters outside of the bedroom, so Scarlett liking it in the car fits the bill, especially if it is a car with the top down.

Chrissy Teigen:

Extra[49] asked Chrissy Teigen and husband, John Legend, to pick a mystery question while they were on the Red Carpet. The question Chrissy selected was to name a public place where they had sex. She asked if that meant the best or worst, and John said best. She then blurted out it was at the Obama thing. So now there's all this speculation that they did it in the White House despite all her protests to the contrary. The *Sports Illustrated* beauty also spilled the beans during a *Cosmopolitan*[50] interview: "We were on our way to Thailand to see my parents, flying commercial first-class. We were under a blanket. We weren't even in one of those pod things. I feel like we should get a trophy for that."

Big adventure loving Sagittarius Chrissy couldn't ask for anything more wild and crazy, White House or not. Any "Obama thing" could make for an exciting time!

Miley Cyrus:

In *Cosmopolitan*[51], Miley Cyrus talked sex toys, especially Ben Wah Balls as being her favorite. She also said that while on her Bangerz Tour, she brought a few things along. In *Elle*[52], she said she felt that she was bringing fans through a sexual awakening, something that the Beatles did in the '60s. She referenced how young girls would sneak out to see Joan Jett, and is happy to be the one that has the appeal now. She added in *The Huffington Post*[53] that she's sad that so many young women base their worth on what they can do for someone sexually, when sex is something beautiful to be shared with the one you love.

Sagittarians know who they are, aren't afraid to do what they want to do, and feel free to express themselves. And Miley is clearly living her Sagittarius life to the fullest.

Sagittarius Celebrity List

November 22:
Rodney Dangerfield
Scarlett Johansson
Billy Jean King
Mark Ruffalo
Sabra Ricci
Hailey Baldwin
Mariel Hemingway
Mads Mikkelsen
Boris Becker
Jamie Lee Curtis
Robert Vaughn

November 23:
Miley Cyrus
Harpo Marx
Nicole "Snooki" Polizzi
Robin Roberts
Maxwell Caulfield
Oded Fehr

November 24:
Sarah Hyland
Katherine Heigl
Billy Connolly
Colin Hanks

November 25:
Billy Burke
Ricardo Montalban

Ben Stein
John F. Kennedy Jr.
Jill Hennessy
Jenna Bush
Christina Applegate
Amy Grant

November 26:
Rita Ora
Charles Schultz
Tina Turner
Kristin Bauer

November 27:
Bruce Lee
Bill Nye
Robin Givens
Jaleel White
Caroline Kennedy
Jimi Hendrix
Victoria Gotti

November 28:
Trey Songz
Judd Nelson
Jon Stewart
Berry Gordy Jr.
Anna Nicole Smith
Ed Harris
Paul Shaffer

November 29:
Howie Mandel
Jeff Fahey
The Game
Anna Faris
Diane Ladd
Don Cheadle
Andrew Mccarthy
Kim Delaney
Chuck Mangione

November 30:
Kaley Cuoco
Ben Stiller
Bo Jackson
Dick Clark
Robert Guillaume
Chrissy Teigen
Clay Aiken
Billy Idol
Mandy Patinkin
Ridley Scott

December 1:
Sarah Silverman
Woody Allen
Richard Pryor
Chanel Iman
Lou Rawls
Bette Midler
Charlene Tilton
Treat Williams

December 2:
Gianni Versace
Lucy Liu
Nelly Furtado
Britney Spears
Daniela Ruah
Monica Seles
Rena Sofer
Stone Phillips

December 3:
Amanda Seyfried
Holly Marie Coombs
Trina Braxton
Ozzy Osbourne
Julianne Moore
Brendan Fraser
Anna Chlumsky
Daryl Hannah
Katarina Witt

December 4:
Jay Z
Jeff Bridges
Marisa Tomei
Fred Durst
Fred Armisen
Tyra Banks
Tony Todd
Max Baer Jr.

December 5:
Frankie Muniz
Walt Disney
Paula Patton
Little Richard
Amy Acker
Margaret Cho
Nick Stahl

December 6:
Debbie Rowe
Tom Hulce
Janine Turner
Judd Apatow
Jobeth Williams

December 7:
Sara Bareilles
Larry Bird
Jennifer Carpenter
C. Thomas Howell
Tom Waits
Johnny Bench
Ellen Burstyn

December 8:
Nicki Minaj
Teri Hatcher
Ian Somerhalder
Kim Basinger
Sammy Davis Jr.
Sinead O'Conner

Gregg Allman
David Carradine
Ann Coulter

December 9:
Redd Foxx
Jakob Dylan
Kirk Douglas
Donny Osmond
Judi Dench
Dick Butkus
Jesse Metcalfe
Felicity Huffman
John Malkovich
Lori Greiner
Beau Bridges
Joan Armatrading

December 10:
Raven Symone
Susan Dey
Bobby Flay
Nia Peeples
Kenneth Branagh
Gloria Loring

December 11:
Nikki Sixx
Mo'Nique
Teri Garr
Rita Moreno
Donna Mills

John Kerry
Mos Def
Jermaine Jackson
Ben Shephard
Gary Dourdan
Carlo Ponti

December 12:
Regina Hall
Frank Sinatra
Jennifer Connelly
Bob Barker
Cathy Rigby
Dionne Warwick
Connie Francis
Sheila E
Madchen Amick
Mayim Bialik

December 13:
Taylor Swift
Christopher Plummer
Jamie Foxx
Nene Leakes
Steve Buscemi
Dick Van Dyke
Ted Nugent
Wendie Malick
Morris Day

December 14:
Vanessa Hudgens
Lee Remick
Miranda Hart
Patty Duke
Kadee Strickland
Dee Wallace Stone
Archie Kao

December 15:
Don Johnson
Adam Brody
Tim Conway
Imani
Dave Clark
Stuart Townsend
Helen Stater
Emily Head
J Paul Getty

December 16:
Benjamin Bratt
Leslie Stahl
Krysten Ritter
Steven Bochco
Jyoti Amge
JB Smoove
Jon Tenney

December 17:
Pope Francis
Bob Guccione
Manny Pacquiao
Milla Jovovich
Sarah Paulson
John Abraham
Duff Goldman
Cailin Russo
Eugene Levy
Giovanni Ribisi
Ernie Hudson
Bill Pullman
Marissa Ribisi
Chris Matthews

December 18:
Sia
Christine Aguilera
DMX
Katie Holmes
Keith Richards
Brad Pitt
Casper Van Dien
Steven Spielberg
Ray Liotta
Steve Austin
Rikki Six
Rachel Griffiths
Ossie Davis

December 19:
Jake Gyllenhaal
Jennifer Beals
Alyssa Milano
Tim Reid
Criss Angel
Cicely Tyson
Reggie White
Paulina Gretzky
Kristy Swanson

December 20:
Jonah Hill
Lucy Pinder
Dick Wolf
John Spencer
Joel Gretsch

December 21:
Samuel L. Jackson
Chris Collins
Kiefer Sutherland
Ray Romano
Jane Fonda
Andy Dick
Jane Kaczmarek
Florence Griffith Joyner
Chris Evert
Phil Donahue
Barry Gordon

CAPRICORN

December 22 – January 19

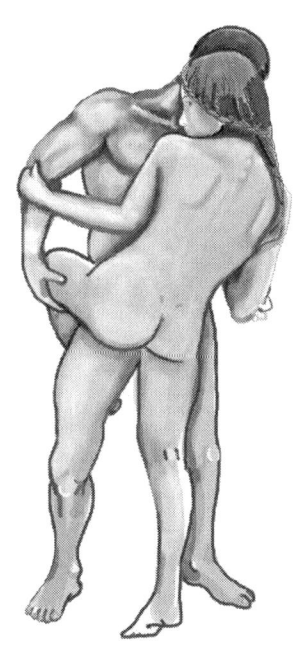

The Executive

December 22-January 19

Capricorn likes to take their time and can be really slow on the uptake. But once things get started, they won't stop until their lover has been well satisfied, maybe more than once. The Goat has the patience of a saint, and while they may not dazzle with fancy moves, they stick to what they know with just the right moves!

Ruling Planet: Saturn
Body Part Ruled: Bones
House Ruled: Tenth, the house of social status, career
Element: Earth
Color: Brown
Stone: Garnet
Key Phrase: I use
Trait: Steadiness
Weakness: Condescending
Quality: Cardinal

What Capricorn Is All About

Some people think I'm cold and they've never even met me. I guess I walk around with a stern look on my face or an invisible sign on my forehead that says: unapproachable. I can't see it when I look in the mirror, but it must be there because I sometimes see people glance in my direction, turn around, and walk away. I don't get it.

I'm a great friend, all my friends will tell you that. I'm the first one they call when they need help. I'm sympathetic and will listen to what's going on with all my friends. I'll even sit down with them and help make a plan when things are falling apart all around them. I'm no fair weather friend; I'm right there until they've got their feet on solid ground. And I do it just because I'm a nice person and it's the right thing to do. No tit for tat for me! It's all about being there for a friend. No expectations and no strings attached.

I can seem gloomy and rigid because I have all this responsibility and am so disciplined. I'm always doing everything by the book. No deviations for me, gotta keep it on the straight and narrow. What would happen if I just broke loose and did something off the wall? Hell if I know! I've never done it. And I never will. Well, maybe I might, but I'd have to weigh the consequences to see if it was worth it. Hey, I'm not a chicken! There's just usually a right and a wrong way to do everything. And

I have to do it the right way; I have to be in control! Some people probably think this is boring, but not I.

I want to feel appreciated. No one would know that because I don't walk around wearing my heart on my sleeve, like some of these other signs. I have to be certain that I can trust someone before I let him or her get a look at my heart. When I know that the person I'm into is trustworthy, I'll make my move. Once I do, you'd better watch out. I'll be so hot, you'll need some aloe vera for those burns I leave behind. Do the words too hot to handle mean anything?

When I make a commitment, that's it. I want it to be for life. I guess I'm like a swan or a wolf in that way; I'm going to mate for life. I'm so loyal I'll stick with you through thick and thin until the end, unless you do something to piss me off, and trust me, you don't want that to happen. There are some things that irritate me, and others, that make me mad as hell. But the only deal breaker is if you cheat on me. Then all my mate-for-life mumbo jumbo will be meaningless, and I'll be yelling "don't let the door hit you in the ass" after throwing out your stuff.

Of course, sometimes I just pretend to be mad so we can have make-up sex. If I really get into it, I can make sure we go at it all night. It might take a while to unleash all this hidden passion, but it will be well worth it. And there's no putting that genie back in the bottle. So once you get me, you've got me for good.

CAPRICORN WOMAN:

The Capricorn woman presents a very cool, almost cold, exterior. She may seem aloof, hard to approach, and all business, which is natural because she has a good head for business. She can climb the ladder to success just as well as her male counterpart, and is quite comfortable sitting at the head of the boardroom table. Making money is something she is good at, not just for the sake of making it, but for her security, so she doesn't have to be dependent on anyone else. She's very independent and wants to keep it that way. So, even when she's in a committed relationship, she will invest any extra funds to ensure her own future.

She has highly skilled leadership qualities and is great at time management, which benefits both her public and personal life. Capricorn can do it all, have the career, the home, and the family. Her management skills help her keep things separated, so nothing infringes on anything else, and all areas of her life get her undivided attention when she's focused on each one. She has a schedule and sticks to it. That's how she makes sure to have one on one time when she's in a relationship; she puts him on the schedule!

The Cap woman can be distant and unemotional, but deep down she has a streak of romance tucked away. Will it be easy to find and bring into the light? It depends on the kind of man you are. She doesn't play hard to get, even if it seems that way. It's a matter of her sizing up the situation to determine if you're even worth her time. Once she's made up her mind, it's going to be all or nothing.

And don't even think about giving her a reason to make her think she made the wrong choice! Any indiscretion or hanky-panky on your part will bring her wrath. It's unforgiveable as well as unforgettable. If you thought *Revenge* was only a TV show, think again! She will make a plan of how to torture you, and when you least expect it, will make her move. Everything will be on her timetable. Remember that schedule she makes and sticks to? How does surgical removal of private body parts next Thursday at midnight sound? If you're going to cheat on a Capricorn woman, think twice, or end the relationship first, and then move on to whoever caught your eye. At least everything will remain intact!

When it comes to sex, this woman is a smoldering keg waiting to be ignited. She goes along with all the foreplay that you want, but will be ready before most other signs. She'll go from zero to sixty in six. That's six seconds flat. Her sexual imagination may leave a little to be desired, but you bring your bag of tricks and she'll be up to the occasion. Her endurance and repeat performances will be outstanding. You best be eating your Wheaties, or you'll never be able to keep up with her.

CAPRICORN MAN:

While some may think Capricorn is a stodgy old Goat, he's really a virile, physical man's man. Think Tom Selleck as the original Marlboro Man. Yeah, I know Capricorns are more comfortable in a suit and tie, than in jeans, chaps, and a cowboy hat on the back of a horse. But it's the image and all that sexy passion that lies beneath the cool Capricorn façade.

The Capricorn man hides his emotions so well; you probably won't even know when he's genuinely and passionately in love. He can be simmering inside, but will make no attempt to tell his ladylove how he feels until he knows what her intentions are. Is it friendship, a roll in the hay, or does she love him back? If it's friendship, he'll just go on being her friend and hide his broken heart. If it's a roll in the hay, and he hadn't already decided she's the one, he'd go for it; he's a man after all. But if he does think she's the one, that would be too painful knowing there would be nothing more, so he'd have to pass and forever keep his feelings to himself. If she loves him back, he'd be singing passionate love songs to her, showing emotions he never thought he had!

He gets a charge from money, not the same charge as sex, but pretty close. He works his ass off to get his money and will stash part of it away for his retirement. But he has an appreciation of rare fine wines, rare books, gourmet foods, and other high quality things, so will allot enough from the budget to be able to indulge at least once in a while.

One of the fastest ways to lose Capricorn is to make him be the butt of your jokes. This is a huge no-no for his ego and self-esteem. He will be gone in a flash, with no turning back. Okay, so you were just teasing. That won't matter. Some things are off limits and that is one of them, probably the number one.

Capricorn has a very healthy sex drive! It is the gift that keeps on giving, and giving, and giving. Okay, there's no turn off switch! Once you turn him on, you'll have the time of your life. He has lots of stamina and can go all night, so be happy that he picked you. You're going to be a happy girl!

EROGENOUS ZONE: The knees and area surrounding them. Placing a hand on the knee grabs the attention of any Capricorn.

SEX POSITION:

The standing wrap around! Having sex on top of a mountain is a fetish both will love.

SEX PROPS:

A XXX video is the perfect prop for both the male and female goat.

Who Gets Them Hot And Not So Much

Hottest Sex: Taurus, Virgo, Scorpio, Pisces

One Night Stand (or Two): Aries, Cancer, Libra, Capricorn

Not So Much: Gemini, Leo, Sagittarius, Aquarius

Capricorn with Aries:

These two start out with lots of excitement in the bedroom and everything surrounding sex. Neither is afraid to ask for what they want, so things can heat up quickly, even without lots of experimentation. What they lack in that area, they make up for in endurance, and will have great workouts that leave them feeling like they're running marathons. But that's where anything that they have in common ends. Both are stubborn and stick to their guns on everything they do. They will spend so much time bickering, they'll quickly forget about the good times they had in the bedroom.

Capricorn with Taurus:

Ecstatic is what these two Earth signs will make each other. Reserved Capricorn needs someone who can unleash his or her pent up emotions and Taurus is just the one to do it. Capricorn likes a lover who's dependable and that's Taurus' middle name. Taurus loves all-nighters and Cap's fortitude will be just what Taurus needs to make that happen. These two get so hot they seem more like Fire signs. And in the bright light of day, they're a matching set. Capricorn loves making money and has everything it takes to get a lot of it. Taurus loves stashing all that cash away for the future. While they both love their creature comforts in and out of the boudoir, they'll make sure they have a big nest egg for their golden years.

Capricorn with Gemini:

These two could save a lot of time and disappointment by not even starting down the primrose path, but most people have to learn the hard way. Gemini's bawdy bedroom talk and wit can get other signs going, but for Capricorn, not so much. The Goat tries to roll with it, but really thinks it's crass and more of a turn-off than turn-on. Gem thinks this attitude is absurd and that Capricorn is an old stick-in-the-mud. In daily life, Capricorn plays by the rules and Gem can't stand them. In fact, Gemini is the first one to break them! So, it's no surprise when the beginning is really the end for these two.

Capricorn with Cancer:

When these two opposites hook up, they'll be setting off fireworks, at least for a few times. Cancer can't get enough of the Goat's advances. Even though Cap's superior attitude about the bump and grind can get tiresome, the frequency keeps the sex-loving Crab more than happy. But out in the real world, Capricorn spends too much time in the boardroom and not enough time reassuring the needy Cancer. Since both back away from confrontations, they'll both never get their needs met, and the Roman candle turns out to be a dud.

Capricorn with Leo:

Leo loves to be adored, thinks everyone should worship the ground they walk on, and can't image why Capricorn isn't into prostrating at the shrine of the Lion. Capricorn finds all this pomp and circumstance to be overbearing and boring. Leo needs lots of romance, and Capricorn is more into corporate dealings, because business is the bottom line even when it comes to sex. Capricorn thinks Leo is crazy and self-centered. Leo thinks Capricorn is about as exciting as staring at the wall. There'll be no big drama when these two end it, because no one is getting too invested in this mess.

Capricorn with Virgo:

On the surface, Virgo comes off as a prude, but underneath has the heart of a sexual dynamo waiting to get the pistons fired up. And Capricorn's slow-and-steady-wins-the-race attitude is just what's needed to rev up that engine! Once these two get going, they won't even notice the checkered flag waving after they've crossed the finish line in first place. When they finally come back to reality, their hard-working tendencies kick in and they start planning a life together. This pair is a sure-fired winner!

Capricorn with Libra:

Libra will have Capricorn all aflame and aroused with their beguiling ways. Capricorn's straightforward approach to sex will have Libra excited and ready for more. But once they leave the temple of bliss, it can get ugly very quickly. Capricorn wants Libra to sign on the bottom line of the in-it-for-life contract, and Libra wants hearts and flowers, luxury, and candlelit dinners. This is a no-win situation, with the contract going through the shredder. They'll be better off storing the sultry memories away on a zip drive and pulling the plug.

Capricorn with Scorpio:

There's no denying the intimate symbiosis between the Scorpion and the Goat, so they may as well turn on all the lights to see what's really going on. They want extreme contact and the big adventure. They need to shut out the rest of the world, so there'll be no interruptions or distractions. Capricorn is less extroverted than Scorpio, but it won't take long for Capricorn's lusty side to forget all about the meaning of introverted. When two such mighty personalities come together, they're bound to have some disagreements. But as long as they don't go for the jugular every time, this can definitely be a lasting match.

Capricorn with Sagittarius:

Like with the other two Fire signs, Aries and Leo, Capricorn is drawn to Sagittarius like a moth to a flame. Only, in this case, they spontaneously combust once they get too close. Sag's enthusiasm and happy-go-lucky ways will turn Capricorn from stoic to bold and assured in a flash. The grumpy Goat can't help but respond to Sagittarius, and will be walking around grinning from ear to ear, for a while! But soon enough, Capricorn will want commitment, honesty, and a deep connection. Sagittarius' "I want my freedom" attitude will piss Capricorn off to no end, and Cap's possessiveness will send Sag running for the hills. So once again, Capricorn will have one to remember on cold winter's nights, but will have to forego the body to keep them warm.

Capricorn with Capricorn:

As with all matches between the same sign, these two Capricorns are mirror images of each other, but they may not love what they see. They will adore each other as best friends. They love doing things together because they'll know what to expect and will want to do the same things. It will be like wearing a comfortable pair of old shoes that they don't want to get rid of, instead of having to break in a new pair. The sex will be comfortable, probably missionary, nothing exciting, but familiar. But who needs familiar? Caps need exciting, someone to get them out of their routine. So, remain best buds and help find each other the perfect match.

Capricorn with Aquarius:

The uptight Wall Street exec and the quintessential flower child! What do they have in common? Absolutely nothing! While this lack of commonality could work for some combos, it won't for Capricorn and Aquarius. Aquarius will think Capricorn is a boring stiff shirt, and Capricorn won't be amused by Aquarius' flowing hippie style. Capricorn's workaholic habits will never mesh with the Aquarius' let's-see-where-the wind-takes-me attitude. This pair may not even be able make good friends, so definitely steer clear of the bedroom!

Capricorn with Pisces:

When first looking at this match, it looks like the grounds of a battlefield. But otherworldly Pisces can actually get Capricorn to reveal, and act on, their inner secret fantasies. This will give Capricorn a respite from all those long days and nights pouring over spreadsheets and business plans. The Capricorn's take-charge actions will have the Fish swimming in circles of ecstasy. Pisces will have the Goat ready to stay on the ethereal plane for a heavenly match. Capricorn can always Skype with the suits and stay with Pisces in the erotic fantasyland they helped create!

Capricorn Celebrities And Dirty, Sexy, Funny

Kate Moss:

Possibly the original Wild Child, waif thin Supermodel, Kate Moss shocked a lot of people before settling into her own sexuality. She shot to fame after a 1993 photo shoot for *British Vogue*[54]. She met Johnny Depp at an after-party following the CFDA awards in 1994, and launched into a frenzy of drugs, sex, and alcohol that went on for four years, until Depp decided he'd had enough. Kate was devastated by the breakup and became enmeshed in what the London tabloids called "the Primrose Hill set", which was made up of rock and movie stars, including Sadie Frost and husband Jude Law. Many have said that Kate and Sadie fell in love and began an affair, even bringing Jude into the mix for threesomes. She nearly lost it all even after apologizing publicly and doing a stint in rehab. She was able to come back from the shame of drugging, alcohol, and sex to reclaim her fame and find love.

Capricorns can become addicted to vices that they think will keep them thin and beautiful, and give them a release from their rigorous schedules. It seems Kate let these vices get the best of her, but like a true Cap, was able to recover and get back to business!

Bradley Cooper:

Bradley Cooper has a long list of beauties that he has dated, including Renee Zellweger, Zoe Saldana, Isabella Brewster, Jennifer Esposito, and possibly Jennifer Aniston, Jennifer Lopez, and Sandra Bullock. The former World's Sexiest Man told *The Mirror.co.UK*[55], that this list doesn't represent conquests, but good old romance. He considers himself to be a die-hard romantic and loves to be with a great woman. While physical beauty is a great asset, he thinks that closeness and harmony are more important. But by no means is he a prude, in fact quite the opposite. This hunk speaks French and recites poetry, which can drive the ladies crazy with big payoffs.

Like most Capricorns, Bradley has been associated with many women. It is common for Capricorn men to "try on" a few, or a lot, of potential partners, before making a commitment. We'll see if Bradley's ready to take the leap anytime soon.

Betty White:

At 93 years young, Betty White still has it going on, as shown in an interview *AARP Magazine*[56]. She said that since husband, Allen Ludden, passed away in 1981, she has been alone, but if he were still alive they would be having sex, lots of sex. She did add that if Robert Redford were available the same would be true! Betty said the secret to a wonderful marriage is enthusiasm. When she knew Allen was coming home soon, she'd freshen up, change her clothes, and redo her makeup. He'd always call and ask her to go on a date with him, which could be dinner at home with romantic music and a little cheek-to-cheek to keep the spark alive. When asked if there was anything she would do differently, she said she wouldn't have married her first two husbands. She then added that they prepared her to know the real deal when Allen came along.

Once a Capricorn has made the decision to have a committed relationship, they'll settle for nothing less. They want the whole enchilada!

Jude Law:

Jude Law has had his share of infamous liaisons over the years, some that he 'fessed up to and some not. As he told *The Guardian*,[57] he would prefer people to forgive and forget affairs like the one with his children's nanny, Daisy Wright, which blew up his relationship with finance Sienna Miller, and caused big problems with ex-wife, Sadie Frost. Back in the day, he and Sadie were said to have been part of the Primrose Hill set of drugs, sex, and alcohol with Kate Moss, and others. He has denied this, but there is much hanging out there that says otherwise. Despite his unfaithful habits, Daisy Wright raved about Judd's sexual virtues and virility in her tell-all book[58], validating the thousands of women who have fantasized about being the one with handsome Judd.

While most Capricorns become monogamous once in a committed relationship, it's not unusual for them to stray if there is dissatisfaction with their partner. Issues like these may have caused Jude's wandering eye. He has made his mea culpa repeatedly, so it's time for him to be let off the hook.

Capricorn Celebrity List

December 22:
Meghan Trainor
Jordin Sparks
Diane Sawyer
Ralph Fiennes
Lady Bird Johnson
Maurice Gibb
Robin Gibb
Diane Sawyer
Ali Lohan
Hector Elizondo
Steve Garvey

December 23:
Eddie Vetter
Susan Lucci
Holly Madison
Corey Haim
Jim Harbaugh
Mallory Hagan
Carla Bruni
Naked Cowboy

December 24:
Ryan Seacrest
Stephenie Meyer
Ricky Martin
Kate Spade
Marr Passmore

Diedrich Bader
Rebecca Crews
Mark Valley

December 25:
Demaryius Thomas
Dido
Sissy Spacek
Emma Stater
Jimmy Buffett
Rod Serling
Annie Lennox
Barbara Mandrell
Conrad Hilton
Chris Rene
Rickey Henderson
Jillie Mack

December 26:
Prodigy
Jared Leto
Kit Harington
John Walsh
Alexander Wang

December 27:
Pleasure P
John Amos
Louis Pasteur

Gerard Depardieu
Eva LaRue
Masi Oka

December 28:
John Legend
Denzel Washington
Maggie Smith
David Archuleta
Seth Meyers
Sienna Miller
Joe Manganiello
Gale King
Nichelle Nichols
Robin McGraw
Vanessa Ferlito
James Foley

December 29:
Slim Jimmy
Jon Voight
Mary Tyler Moore
Mekhi Phifer
Jude Law
Ted Danson
Jon Voight
Jane Levy
Katherine Moennig
Patricia Clarkson
Alexa Ray Joel

December 30:
LeBron James
Ellie Goulding
Matt Lauer
Tyrese Gibson
Tracey Ullman
Laila Ali
Tiger Woods
Meredith Veira
Sandy Koufax
Patti Smith
Bo Diddley
Daniel Sunjata

December 31:
Psy
Donna Summer
Gabby Douglas
Anthony Hopkins
Val Kilmer
John Denver
Donna Summer
Sam Faiers
Ben Kingsley
Henri Matisse
Dian von Furstenberg
Bebe Neuwirth
James Remar
Lance Reddick

January 1:
Colin Morgan
Morris Chestnut
Meryl Davis
Tank
Verne Mini-Me Troyer
Cat Cora
JD Salinger
Elin Nordegren

January 2:
Karina Smirnoff
Cuba Gooding Jr.
Tia Carrere
Dax Shepard
Kate Bosworth
Paz Vego
Jack Hanna
Christy Turlington
Anna Lee

January 3:
Eli Manning
Victoria Principal
JRR Tolkien
Mel Gibson
Danica McKeller
James Marsden
Stephen Stills
Robert Loggia
Dabney Coleman

January 4:
Graham Elliot
Dyan Cannon
Labrinth
Tina Knowles
Louis Braille
Vanity
Michael Stipe
Patty Loveless
Floyd Patterson
Don Shula
Julia Ormond

January 5:
Bradley Cooper
Diane Keaton
January Jones
Pamela Sue Martin
Carrie Ann Inaba
Marilyn Manson
Clancy Brown
Robert Duvall
Suki Waterhouse
Kristin Cavallari

January 6:
Rowan Atkinson
Eddie Redmayne
Nancy Lopez
Julie Chen
Joey Lauren Adams

Nigella Lawson
Ree Drummond
Danny Thomas
Howie Long
Danny Pintauro
Nancy Lopez

January 7:
Jeremy Renner
Katie Couric
Aloe Blacc
Nicholas Cage
David Caruso
Dustin Diamond
Butterfly McQueen
Kenny Loggins
John Rich

January 8:
R Kelly
Stephen Hawking
David Bowie
Elvis Presley
Shirley Bassey
Ami Dolenz
Carolina Herrera
Bob Eubanks
Yvette Mimieux

January 9:
Kate Middleton
Dave Matthews
Jimmy Page
Dave Matthews
Crystal Gayle
Bart Starr
Mathew Knowles
JK Simmons
Joan Baez

January 10:
Rod Stewart
George Foreman
Jim Croce
Sal Mineo
Pat Benetar
Sarah Shahi
Frank Sinatra Jr.
Linda Lovelace

January 11:
Mary J Blige
Naomi Judd
Amanda Peet
Kim Coles
Lindsay Arnold

January 12:
Jana Duggar
Joe Frazier

Howard Stern
John Lasseter
Ray Price
Oliver Platt
Kirstie Alley

January 13:
Liam Hemsworth
Gwen Verdon
Orlando Bloom
Julia Louis-Dreyfus
Patrick Dempsey
Trace Adkins
Shonda Rhimes
Penelope Ann Miller
Michael Pena

January 14:
Dave Grohl
Faye Dunaway
LL Cool J
Jason Bateman
Jack Jones
Carl Weathers
Holland Taylor
Andy Rooney

January 15:
Pitbull
Martin Luther King Jr.
Drew Brees

Regina King
Chad Lowe
Charo
Lloyd Bridges
Eddie Cahill
Ronnie Van Zant
Mario Van Peebles
Paulina Vega
Sophie Sumner
Randy White

January 16:
Sade
Ronnie Milsap
Kate Moss
Joe Flacco
John Carpenter
Debbie Allen
AJ Foyt
Aaliyah

January 17:
Betty White
Eartha Kitt
Michelle Obama
Jim Carrey
Muhammad Ali
Susanna Hoffs
Steve Harvey
Zooey Deschanel
Ray J

Kid Rock
James Earl Jones
Andy Kaufman
Maksim Chmerkovskiy
Maury Povich
Naveen Andrews
Vidal Sassoon

Tippi Hedren
Paul Cezanne
Junior Seau

January 18:
Jason Segel
Cary Grant
Kevin Costner
Jesse L Martin

January 19:
Jodie Sweetin
Dolly Parton
Lil Scrappy
Jean Stapleton
Shawn Johnson
Janis Joplin
Shawn Wayans
Paula Deen
Paul Rodriquez
Katey Sagal
Phil Everly
Michael Crawford
Pasha Kovalev
Desi Arnaz Jr.
Robert Palmer

$\mathcal{A}$QUARIUS

January 20 – February 18

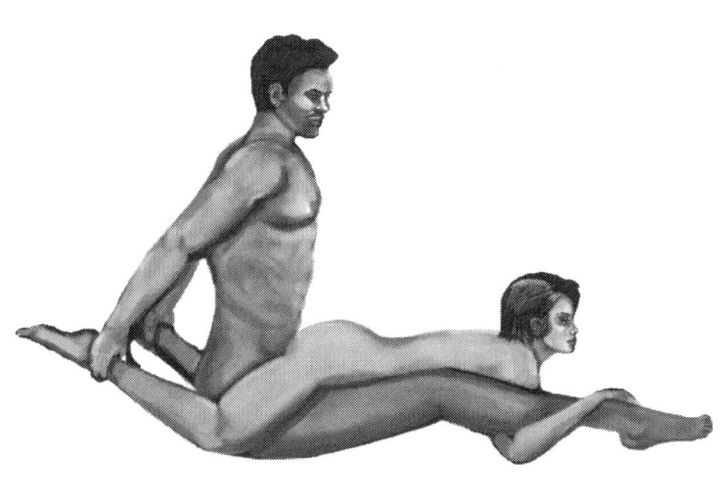

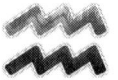

The Intellectual

January 20-February 18

Aquarius is the big experimenter of the zodiac, so they will have all the latest tricks up their sleeve. If the thought of an overloading stash of sex toys is distasteful to any of the other signs, Aquarius won't make a good match as their main squeeze. But for those who are into it, the Water Bearer will take them places they've never been.

Symbol: The Water Bearer
Ruling Planet: Uranus
Body Part Ruled: Circulatory system
House Ruled: Eleventh, the house of friends, acquaintances, detached relationships, societies
Element: Air
Color: Bright Blue
Stone: Amethyst
Key Phrase: I know
Trait: Friendliness
Weakness: Aloof
Quality: Fixed

What Aquarius Is All About

Don't try to hold me down, because I won't stand for it. I have to be free to go it on my own. My independence is crucial to me; it's like my life's blood. Without it, I may as well wither up. Yeah, I know that I come across as being all cool and aloof like nothing ever bothers me, but that's just because I keep my emotions close to the vest.

I'm a known rebel, and sometimes I act out just to stir up shit. Of course, my way of acting out isn't the same as others. I don't pitch a fit or throw a tantrum; in fact, most people wouldn't even know I was rebelling. They would just think I'd gone further into aloof mode, or that I was a stone-cold bitch. But it's not to worry, because I can talk my way out of anything. I talk to anyone and everyone about anything! I'm a great conversationalist, if I say so myself, and I do. Give me 5 minutes and I'll turn anyone who thought I was a bitch into my biggest fan.

I'm very intelligent and know just the right things to say to get you on my side, but I would never do that. I have my opinions and can be really stubborn about them, but I'd never cram them down your throat. I hold our differences in the highest regard, so while I could say all the perfect things to sway how you feel about anything, I won't do it. I reserve that for when I'm trying to further one of my causes about human rights or environmental issues.

That's when I really get going. I could sell ice to an Eskimo, and have raised large amounts of money for charities and other organizations just with my verbal gift. I am very persuasive and tug at the heartstrings, and the purse strings, until people are fully supportive.

I have a great sense of humor and can be very witty, not just in general, but in the bedroom as well. Sex for me is enjoyable, entertaining, and fun. I'm not into the serious, ardent, or sensitive experience. I want offbeat and creative. Planning every little detail for getting it on is boring to me; I want spontaneity. If the mood strikes me, I want to strike while the iron is hot. And I am hot. Underneath this cool exterior, there's heat, enough to melt away the ice princess or ice prince façade in a flash.

If you want to hop in the sack with me, you'd better be ready to joke around and laugh, a lot. It's so much better to make a game of it, to laugh at each other and with each other. That's what keeps everything fresh and alive. I don't want boring at all, that's when I turn off, tune out, and go back into the aloof condition. And you don't want that. If I'm not having fun, you sure as hell won't be either! So for the time of your life, make me laugh, take out all the stops, and show me what you've got in your bag of tricks. And did I say make me laugh?

AQUARIUS WOMAN:

The Aquarius woman is one of the more independent ones of the zodiac. You won't find her being clingy or pining away after some guy. She's just not into all that emotional drama and takes on a cool detached persona. But she's a dichotomy in a lot of ways, especially because she loves to talk and to connect on a very personal level. Aquarius will talk to anyone, the butcher, the baker, and strangers on the street if they intrigue her.

She is witty and can be entertaining at any party, from the smallest get together to a ballroom filled to the brim. Taking command of any room is her forte. It's also the tool she uses for pursuing humanitarianism around the world. She has a great belief in the equality of all humankind and, as a visionary, will do whatever it takes to enlighten everyone she comes into contact with about the plight of the less fortunate.

When it comes to whom she wants as a lover, she will couple with anyone she finds fascinating until she goes for *the* one. The big L-O-V-E word can cause her to go slightly bananas until she is certain she is ready for it. So, in the meanwhile, she doesn't let her emotions get the best of her; actually she never lets that happen, as she always puts up that cold front if someone is trying to get too close, too fast. When she makes up her mind about a man, she'll go for it. He will have to be alluring and amusing, alluring to catch her interest and amusing to keep her interest and make her laugh. Since she can easily detach from her personal world and move into rescuing the world, laughter is very important for keeping her grounded.

So if you are interested in an Aquarius woman, don't let her slip away to save everyone else, but keep her focused on you. She can be capricious and loves excitement, so she'll need to be wooed, charmed, and courted. Although very futuristic in her thinking, she is into old time chivalry and wants to be treated like a lady. So treat her the way she wants and you'll be half way to a relationship home run. Once she trusts you, she will open up. And to please her in the bedroom, you need to bring all your skills, change it up, and keep it exciting. She'll respond, by rocking your world. Just remember to make her laugh along the way!

AQUARIUS MAN:

The Aquarius man is on a mission to find wisdom and expand his already brilliant mind. He loves to sit back and observe as much as possible to incorporate into that big brain of his. He already has an air of aloofness and detachment about him, so when he is on an info-gathering streak, he will come off as even more distant. Never one to let emotions cloud his actions, the Aquarius man disdains emotional outbursts and is turned off by anyone who goes around emoting all the time.

Sometimes Aquarius feels like he doesn't fit in with others, almost as if he's an alien from another planet. This is because of his progressive life views; so if he doesn't connect with you on an intellectual or mental level, give it time for him to come down to Earth. And if he doesn't, you may as well forget about making any moves beyond friendship. One thing that will not work at all, whether you are friends or trying to make it more, is for you to try to box him in or put a label on him. This is an untraditional man, who follows no rules except his own, and is independent beyond words.

He has communication skills for days, and can literally talk for just as long. He'll carry this into the bedroom, so if you're someone who prefers your sexual encounters to be intensely passionate and quiet, he's definitely not your man. Like his female counterpart, he thinks that sex is a game to be played with humor, wit, and laughter. No, that doesn't mean he's a game-player, he's just into having lots of fun when he's having sex.

He's more of a slow starter than the Aquarius woman and loves lots of foreplay, but once he's ready to get going, he can keep it going for a long, long time. He's into controlling himself until you are ready to join him in the happy ending. So expect amazing surprises that can take your breath away! If you win his heart, be trustworthy, and he'll be faithfully yours. You'll spend the rest of your life full of smiles and laughs.

EROGENOUS ZONE:

The calves and the ankles. A foot massage is nice for other signs, but it needs to include the ankles and calves to get the Aquarius' interest.

SEX POSITION:

Him, seated legs stretched out straight in front of him. Her, lying on her stomach on top of his legs, facing away from him, legs extended behind him. He gets to lean back and hold her ankles, while she wraps her arms around his calves! Aquarius' top fetish is phone sex.

SEX PROPS:

Phallic-shaped sex toys.

Who Gets Them Hot And Not So Much

Hottest Sex: Aries, Gemini, Libra, Sagittarius, Aquarius

One Night Stand (or Two): Leo, Scorpio, Pisces

Not So Much: Taurus, Cancer, Virgo, Capricorn

Aquarius with Aries:

These two are a mixed bag. Aries loves being in charge all the time, which is a bone of contention for Aquarius. But Aries responds well to Aquarius' imaginative and creative moves. If the Ram can subdue their over-the-top need for control, Aquarius would be willing to stick around. The sex will be off the charts, so it is worth a compromise if they can possibly come to terms with that. It doesn't mean Aries has to turn over the power seat to Aquarius, but they do need to share once in a while. If that's a no-go, Aquarius will be the out the door while Aries is still trying to be the boss.

Aquarius with Taurus:

Taurus feels that sex is an integral part of being in a relationship, while the relationship is what's important to Aquarius, with sex being secondary. That's not to say that Aquarius doesn't like sex, they do, but they get caught up in talking about it almost as much as doing it. This paring can be a couple as odd as Oscar and Felix without all the mess. Down to earth Taurus can't understand why Aquarius is so out there in the way they do everything. And Aquarius thinks Taurus is dull with no imagination. Chances are they won't make it to a romp, but if they do, it will be one boring time. No way on this one.

Aquarius with Gemini:

Aquarius and Gemini are the Chatty Cathys of the Zodiac. They'll go on and on about anything, and Gemini's bound to turn the conversation to sex sooner or later, probably sooner rather than later! And Aquarius will jump right in. Both signs are up for anything wild and kinky, and what they haven't done, they'll invent with their genius minds right there in the middle of the act. They are both fun to be around and can be the life of any party. All their many friends will have them on speed-dial for invites to the latest and greatest bash. They will gladly accept, have a ball, and at the end of the night, go home to a party for two!

Aquarius with Cancer:

These two may make it through a one-night stand, but it may be better if they didn't. First off, Aquarius loves talking and will engage anyone within earshot. Jealousy rears its ugly head in Cancer's mind, because they will be certain that Aquarius is looking for someone to hook up with. Sure, if Cancer and Aquarius can make it to that one time fling, it will be hot, and Aquarius will do things Cancer has never experienced before. But in the bright light of day, Aquarius will forget to ring up Cancer with words of assurance and love. Cancer will be crushed and think that Aquarius is heartless. So to avoid all the drama, don't even go there.

Aquarius with Leo:

If Aquarius and Leo could only stay in the bedroom for the rest of their lives, this could be a great match. Leo loves every kinky thing that Aquarius comes up with, while Leo's sensuality and star quality lifestyle turn Aquarius on to no end. But leave the bedroom they must; they do have to work, eat, and pay their bills. That's when the problems start for this passionate pair. Aquarius wants to pursue humanitarian efforts around the world, while the Lion wants to sit back and oversee his or her kingdom. The fundamental differences between these two are a disaster in the making. So they should stick to the bedroom for the good times and then go their separate ways.

Aquarius with Virgo:

When they said that great minds think alike, they weren't talking about Aquarius and Virgo. Although both are highly intelligent and run their lives based on logic rather than emotions, that's as far as it goes. Aquarius has social butterfly tendencies, while Virgo wants to stay at home with a few close friends. Virgo works hard to be successful and Aquarius intellectualizes working hard. Their approaches to sex mirror their philosophies about work. Aquarius can be aloof and disconnected at times, even in the hottest situation. Virgo wants to have the intense, staring into each other's eyes, going to the dark spiritual side, while Aquarius doesn't relate on that deep level. They make great friends, but should find others to get hot and heavy with.

Aquarius with Libra:

Libra will get things heated up for Aquarius in ways they didn't think possible. Libra, the diplomat, knows just what to say and do to get Aquarius to cave in when they're being stubborn, from what movie to see to what position they're going to do. But that's going to be the only issue that these two will have because they are hot, hot for each other. They both have the gift for gab and will spend endless hours talking, especially when they are making sweet love. They may have to make an effort to take the initiative to not let things get boring because that would be a relationship killer. Both can be rather laid back in the assertion department, but both are highly creative, so there's not too much chance that they will succumb to boredom.

Aquarius with Scorpio:

In their bedroom rendezvous, Aquarius and Scorpio will be on each other like white on rice, in fact, they won't be able to tell where one of them ends and the other begins. These two could be accused of being addicted to love, but it's sex that these two really can't get enough of, to the point that they may have to call their chiropractors. Once they come out for air, it will soon become painful in other ways. Aquarius can go into reserved mode, which pisses off the sensitive Scorpio. It's better for these two to find their vice elsewhere, before they realize they can't stand each other.

Aquarius with Sagittarius:

Both Aquarius and Sagittarius love freedom, travel, people, and sex, not necessarily in that order. So this all makes for a good match that can be a lasting one. They both are willing to give each other lots of space, and think sex is the best way to spend a lazy morning, afternoon, or night. They'll love sailing off to Bora Bora to have sex on the white sand beach during their big adventure. Between sexual escapes, they'll have deep, spiritual conversations, because of their forward thinking personalities. Expect this relationship to go the distance!

Aquarius with Capricorn:

The chance of Aquarius and Capricorn getting to the bedroom is pretty much non-existent. Capricorn will be critical of everything Aquarius does, and think they're a major airhead, while Aquarius will think the Goat is an old fart. If they do manage to slip between the sheets, it's not going to rock the world. The only shaking going on will be if an earthquake hits at the same time. Capricorn wants command of the whole world and Aquarius wants to save it. Any serious interactions they have will end in arguments. Capricorn will want to call all the shots and Aquarius will just want to shoot the Goat. Enough said!

Aquarius with Aquarius:

Aquarius and Aquarius. A heavenly match made on another plane! These two will go to great lengths to keep variety in the bedroom, no boring missionary for them. They need excitement and mental stimulation, in fact, the mental aspect of sex may be just as important to them as the physical. They can, and will, play out more sexual fantasies than possibly any other pairing. When it comes to trust, once these two have made the commitment to each other, it's a binding contract. There's no need to worry about either cheating, because it's just not going to happen. They have too much fun together to have to go back to the drawing board.

Aquarius with Pisces:

Aquarius will be fascinated by Pisces' old-fashioned charm when they first meet. Pisces will be an eager participant when Aquarius promises to take the Fish to peaks of pleasure, with their innovative sexual style. Regrettably, that peak will quickly descend into a valley, almost instantaneously. Pisces will go into clingy, tell-me-that-you-love-me mode, which is a bigger turn off for Aquarius than lightning hitting a transformer. Aquarius just isn't into all that daily mushy stuff that Pisces wants, so this isn't going anywhere!

Aquarius Celebrities And Dirty, Sexy, Funny

Rosamund Pike:

Not only did Rosamund Pike have to shoot a sex scene with Neil Patrick Harris 36 times in *Gone Girl*, she had to slit his throat at the same time. They rehearsed for three days before they started shooting. She told *Glamour*[59] that while it was uncomfortable filming over and over, they were able to get through it with humor. She went from intense scenes with Ben Affleck, who played her husband, to dark ones with Neil, who played her ex. They ended up spending a lot of time laughing in the editing room, even at the hot steamy scenes, to loosen up a little.

The laughter around the sex scenes is just what an Aquarius would do in real life, because that is what's important to them. Omitting the murder part, of course.

Bill Maher:

When asked who his teenage fantasy girl was in an interview with *Elle Magazine*[60], Bill Maher said that it had to be

I Dream of Jeannie's Barbara Eden. He said there weren't any midriff tops other than her's shown on TV during the 60's. And he thought the only reason it was okay for her was because she's basically a puff of smoke, and you can't get it on with smoke. He also spoke about his feeling surrounding when a woman withholds sex, saying that he doesn't have the patience to stick around through that. When asked about how it felt to kiss someone with a lip ring, he said that he likes piercings, especially tongue rings, and what the woman can do with that metal.

Aquarians have a thing about otherworldliness, which explains Bill's thing for the Genie! They are also into kink, which ties into his feelings about metal, piercings, and rings!

Rebel Wilson:

On the *Tonight Show*[61], Rebel Wilson talked about her first sex scene in the movie *Pain and Gain*. The director said that they needed to spice things up a bit, so a pair of numchucks that Rebel happened to bring on set made an interesting appearance in the scene. Between takes, she introduced onscreen lover, Anthony Mackie, to Spanx, and did a lot of laughing. On the *Dailymail.com*[62], Rebel talked about doing all her aerial stunts for her upcoming movie *Pitch Perfect 2*, after training with Cirque Du Soleil for five weeks.

Aquarius likes to use props in the bedroom, so what better toys could have been used in the movie but Rebel's own numchucks! They also like roleplaying or doing acrobatics, so she is right on point with doing her own stunt work.

Ashton Kutcher:

On *Pro.Boxoffice.com*[63], Aston Kutcher was asked about how difficult it is to do sex scenes and what he does to get through them. He said he takes a cue from Sir Lawrence Olivier. He starts by saying something to his acting partner to the effect of that he apologizes if he gets aroused and he apologizes if he doesn't get aroused. Then, he hopes he doesn't have to pretend that nothing happened. When he spoke in Sydney, Australia at the *Lenovo Tech My Way*[64] conference, he couldn't help but gush over fiancée Mila Kunis. He told the audience how lucky he is that he gets to be with her and have sex with her.

The fact that Ashton makes light of the bedroom scenes by saying something funny to his co-star reflects on the Aquarius bedroom sense of humor. And like any red-blooded Aquarius, who has made the commitment to be with his ladylove, he can't help but talk about the sex and how great it is. Aquarius will talk about anything to anyone!

Aquarius Celebrity List

January 20:
George Burns
David Lynch
Paul Staley
Buzz Aldrin
Rainn Wilson
Stacey Dash
Melissa Rivers
Bill Maher
Lorenzo Lamas
DeForest Kelly
James Denton
Skeet Ulrich
Federico Fellini
Arte Johnson

January 21:
Jerry Trainor
Geena Davis
Mac Davis
Emma Lee Bunton
Jack Nicklaus
Benny Hill
Billy Ocean
Christian Dior
Placido Domingo
Robby Benson
Telly Savalas
Wolfman Jack

January 22:
Ray Rice
Linda Blair
Guy Fieri
Michael Hutchence
John Hurt
Diane Lane
Logic
Sam Cooke
Bill Bixby
Piper Laurie
Larry Birkhead
Balthazar Getty

January 23:
Mariska Hargitay
Richard Dean Anderson
Tiffany Thiessen
Princess Caroline of
   Monaco
Chesley Sullenberger
Rutger Hauer
Chita Rivera

January 24:
Ernest Borgnine
John Belushi
Neil Diamond
Nastasia Kinski

Mary Lou Retton
Tatyana Ali
Mischa Barton
Sharon Tate
Maria Tallchief
Michio Kaku
Aaron Neville
Oral Roberts

January 25:
Alicia Keys
Pooh Man
Etta James
Ana Ortiz
Steve Prefontaine
Mia Kirshner
Dean Jones
Princess Charlene of
    Monaco
Marcus Samuelsson

January 26:
Paul Newman
Wayne Gretzky
Anita Baker
Eddie Van Halen
Louis Zamperini
Ellen DeGeneres
Angela Davis
Gilles Marini

Scott Glenn
Lucinda Williams

January 27:
Louis Carroll
Bridget Fonda
Mimi Rogers
Rosamund Pike
Alan Cumming
Daisy Lowe
Mikhail Baryshnikov
Cris Collinsworth
Tracy Lawrence
Hannah Teter
James Cromwell

January 28:
Nick Carter
Sarah McLachlan
Alan Alda
Elijah Wood
Joey Fatone
Barbi Benton

January 29:
Adam Lambert
John Forsythe
Harriet Tubman
Heather Graham
Tom Selleck
Oprah Winfrey

Riff Raff
Greg Louganis
Sara Gilbert
Andrew Keegan
Lisa Ramos
Sam Trammell
Katharine Ross
John D. Rockefeller Jr.
Ann Jillian
Edward Burns

January 30:
Christian Bale
Phil Collins
Wilmer Valderrama
Brett Butler
Gene Hackman
Dorothy Malone
Vanessa Redgrave
Jody Watley
Elsa Martinelli

January 31:
Justin Timberlake
Suzanne Pleshette
Jackie Robinson
Minnie Driver
Kerry Washington
Portia de Rossi
Nolan Ryan
Fat Mike

Ernie Banks
Jean Simmons
Anna Silk
Carol Channing
Bobby Moynihan
Kelly Lynch
Glynn Turman

February 1:
Harry Styles
Lisa Marie Presley
Michael C. Hall
Brandon Lee
Clark Gable
Sherman Helmsley
Rick James
Garrett Morris
Pauly Shore
Princess Stephanie of
  Monaco
Rachelle Lefevre
Don Everly
Skylar Laine

February 2:
Shakira
Michael T. Weiss
Tom Smothers
Farrah Fawcett
Ina Garten
Christine Brinkley

Brent Spiner
Emily Rose
Ayn Rand
Graham Nash
Elaine Stritch
Liz Smith

February 3:
Rebel Wilson
Fran Tarkenton
Isla Fisher
Morgan Fairchild
Warwick Davis
Nathan Lane
Amal Alamuddin
Blythe Danner
Maura Tierney
Bob Griese

February 4:
Gavin Degraw
Rosa Parks
Lawrence Taylor
Alice Cooper
Natalie Imbruglia
Oscar De La Hoya
Gabrielle Anwar
Clint Black
David Brenner
Betty Friedan

February 5:
Henry Hank Aaron
Barbara Hershey
Bobby Brown
H. R. Giger
Sara Evens
Jennifer Jason Leigh
Michael Sheen
Roger Staubach
Tim Meadows
Laura Linney
Barbara Hershey
Jennifer Jason Leigh
Red Buttons

February 6:
Bob Marley
Natalie Cole
Ronald Reagan
Kris Humphries
Axl Rose
Zsa Zsa Gabor
Fabian
Tom Brokaw
Rip Torn
Kathy Najimy
Robert Townsend
Mamie Van Doren

February 7:
Aston Kutcher
Chris Rock
Laura Ingalls Wilder
Garth Brooks
James Spader
Isaiah Thomas
Eddie Izzard
Tina Majorino
Sinclair Lewis
Miguel Ferrer

February 8:
Bethany Hamilton
Gary Coleman
James Dean
Seth Green
Gary Coleman
Pooch Hall
John Williams
Lana Turner
Nick Nolte
John Grisham
Jack Lemmon
Mary Steenburgen

February 9:
Judith Light
Joe Pesci
Carol King
Mia Farrow

Travis Tritt
Charles Shaughnessy
Alice Walker
Gypsy Rose Lee
Amber Valletta
Amrita Singh

February 10:
Chloe Grace Moretz
Emma Roberts
Elizabeth Banks
George Stephanopoulos
Jimmy Durante
Laura Dern
Robert Wagner
Paul Hollywood
Mark Spitz
Roberta Flack
Leontyne Price
Vince Gilligan
Greg Norman

February 11:
Kelly Rowland
Sheryl Crow
Taylor Lautner
Jennifer Aniston
Burt Reynolds
Brandy Norwood
Natalie Dormer
Matt Lawrence

Leslie Nielsen
Damian Lewis
Eva Gabor

February 12:
Bill Russell
Judy Blume
Josh Brolin
Arsenio Hall
Michael McDonald
Christina Ricci
Chynna Phillips
Joanna Kerns
Aaron Sanchez

February 13:
Jerry Springer
George Segal
Prince Michael Jackson
Peter Gabriel
Stockard Channing
Mike Krzyzewski
Kelly Hu
Peter Tork
Mena Suvari
Chuck Yeager
Kim Novak
Oliver Reed
Neal Mcdonough

February 14:
Tiffany Thornton
Meg Tilly
Florence Henderson
Drew Bledsoe
Jim Kelly
Jack Benny
Enrico Colantoni
Big Smo
Gregory Hines
Teller

February 15:
Chris Farley
Jane Seymour
Harvey Korman
Matt Goening
Janice Dickinson
Greer Grammer
John Barrymore
Doda
Melissa Manchester
Michael Easton

February 16:
Patty Andrews
Ice-T
Sonny Bono
LaVar Burton
John McEnroe
Jim Cantore

Margaux Hemingway
William Katt
James Ingram

Juice Newton
Jack Palance
Sarah Brown
Jess Walton

February 17:
Michael Jordan
Rene Russo
Ed Sheeran
Bryan White
Paris Hilton
Denise Richards
Larry the Cable Guy
Jason Ritter
Joseph Gordon-Levitt
Jim Brown
Lou Diamond Phillips
Mary Ann Mobley
Jerry O'Connell
Hal Holbrook

February 18:
John Travolta
Vanna White
Dr Dre
Matt Dillon
Molly Ringwald
Yoko Ono
Jillian Michaels
Toni Morrison
Cybill Shepherd
George Kennedy

PISCES

February 19 – March 20

The Crusader

February 19-March 20

Pisces wants the emotional connection when it comes to their sex life. They are the big dreamers of the zodiac, so their fantasy of the experience is just as important to them as the actual physical act. Anyone interested in the Fish will either have to take charge or let Pisces take them on the Magical Mystery Tour of the Cosmos. Either way, it should be a great joyride!

Symbol: Two Fish
Ruling Planet: Neptune
Body Part Ruled: Immune system
House Ruled: Twelfth, the house of endings, collective unconscious, secrets, spirituality
Element: Water
Color: Sea Green
Stone: Aquamarine
Key Phrase: I believe
Trait: Compassion
Weakness: Escapism
Quality: Mutable

What Pisces Is All About

Some people think that I am rather strange, and I suppose it's true. I have one foot in the real world and the other in the spirit world. To just say this out loud around other people can be really weird. They start to look at me like I'm some kind of freak, which is so far from the truth.

Okay, I'll admit to being eccentric in some ways, but freaky doesn't jibe with who I am, unless you're talking bedroom antics. One of the big things is that I'm very intuitive and can sense what's going on around me, including with all the people I come in contact with. So I can pick up on all the stuff they're thinking about me, in fact I can *hear* the words on the instinctual level.

When people really get to know me, they can see how spiritual and sensitive I am, and how easily my feelings get hurt. With all my otherworldly connections, I should always be on top of whom to stay away from and whom I should hang out with. Most of the time I'm spot on, but there's always that illusion and delusion thing that I have to deal with, so sometimes I get confused and my radar is off kilter.

When it comes to whom I'm hot for, I really do use my intuition to make sure we're going to be compatible before I do anything to draw attention to myself. I usually don't make the first move, but I have my ways of letting the one know that I'm interested or at least available. I don't do anything directly, like walking up and saying "hey hot stuff, wanna buy me a drink?" Oh no, that's for other loose type signs.

I have some seductive moves, but they're so subtle, most don't even realize I've got my game face on. That's the beauty of it all, Neptune, my ruler, let's me be whoever I want to be. That's also why I like role-playing so much in the bedroom. I can be the French maid, the naughty nurse, or a ride 'em cowgirl! Or I can be Little Red Riding Hood and you can be the Wolf. Oh, please don't eat me, Mr. Wolf. Wink, wink!

I can be voracious in the bedroom, but you will have to initiate what we do. I will be right there with you, but I just can't be the one to start anything. Once I know that what we have is real, I will be so loyal and faithful. I will make it my mission to make sure you are happy. But there will be times that I have to leave; no I don't mean that I will physically leave, but as I have one foot in both the physical and spiritual realms, I have to spend some time in meditation and contemplation.

But I'll be back soon and will share with you everything I learn, so we can be on the same page and make our connection even stronger. Both in and out of the bedroom.

PISCES WOMAN:

The Pisces woman is exceptionally intuitive, maybe more than any other sign, except Scorpio. Don't think that you can pull the wool over her eyes, because it just isn't going to happen. She is very sensitive and caring when it comes to her friends. She makes every effort to help a friend who is in need, whether it is to help them move or to just sit with them when a family member is in the emergency room.

Pisces has the tendency to take on the problems of close friends as if they were her own because of her sensitivity. While this is admirable, she actually can feel their pain and become so enmeshed in the issues that it becomes difficult to separate whose problem it really is. She wants to make everything better for those she cares about, to her own detriment. If you have a Pisces friend and you can see that she is about to go full throttle to rectify whatever problem you have going on, don't let them as, in the long run, you will be doing them a disservice. Instead just let her be there to comfort you, hold your hand, or listen while you vent. And remember that she's going to be a lifelong friend.

The Pisces woman's personality may be elusive and hard to pinpoint as she has a mysterious side that can keep you guessing. She can be very much like a chameleon and take on aspects of her surroundings. When she changes environments, she will also change, making her something of a shape-shifter. But one thing's for sure; she'll always be interesting.

This carries over to the bedroom, where she will keep you on your toes. She is soft, feminine, and enchanting. She can also be seductive in subtle ways that make her seem like a tease. Her glyph, two fish swimming in opposite directions, tells it all in some ways. All soft on one side, and sexual catch of the decade on the other.

There likely won't be anything she won't do when the two of you get down to it, if you ask. The answer will be a resounding yes, but you have to ask!

PISCES MAN:

The Pisces man is more unpredictable than his female counterpart, even though she is a chameleon. He is a romantic, but can be reputed to be a bit of a womanizer. So anyone who loves a Pisces man may have to keep an eye on him. But if you know how to handle him, you can mold him into anything you want him to be.

He definitely won't be the businessman that Capricorn is, but he excels at writing and could be a great author. Anything in the Arts, poetry, acting, or musical will be lucrative for him. So there's no worry that he can't support himself or his loved ones. Besides, there's always the chance that he will sing to you, or recite a romantic poem while he's making love to you.

If you really want to impress him, let him teach you something in a subject that is near and dear to his heart. He loves anything to do with the paranormal and spiritual side of life. If you aren't well versed, or not quite a true believer, seek out your nearest psychic, Madame whoever, and have a reading so you can at least relate to this enlightened creature. It will give the two of you something to talk about and can be lots of fun.

He is the kind of man who is great for any woman who thinks that men are just insensitive boors. He is very sensitive, to the point that he can be hurt easily, but would probably never show it because he does have a sense of pride around appearing too vulnerable. He's going to go the extra mile to make sure you are happy and well satisfied. Pisces is excellent when it comes to making love, and is very old school about it. He's one of, or possibly the only man of the zodiac, who feels you should have an out of body experience when having sex. So if you want a love match with bedroom antics that are completely out of this world, Pisces is the man for you!

EROGENOUS ZONE:

The feet. Pampering the feet is heavenly for Pisces.

SEX POSITION:

Her, lying back on the edge of the bed. Him, standing, one foot on bed, so she can play with his foot. She hooks one leg over his knee and he holds her other foot, so he can nibble on her toes. The fish has a toe fetish, both sucking on them and having theirs sucked.

SEX PROPS: The Kama Sutra is great for Pisces, because they are up for anything.

Who Gets Them Hot And Not So Much

Hottest Sex: Aries, Cancer, Scorpio, Capricorn

One Night Stand (or Two): Taurus. Libra, Aquarius, Pisces

Not So Much: Gemini, Leo, Virgo, Sagittarius

Pisces with Aries:

Aries' take-charge attitude will grab Pisces' interest from the get go. Since Pisces can be into submission, they'll gladly acquiesce to Aries' domination. Pisces uses imaginative techniques to keep Aries interested. Getting down to the nitty-gritty of the situation is never a problem for these two. The only issue will be whether Aries can learn to keep their big mouths closed or at least censor their words, so they don't say something harsh to hurt sensitive Pisces' feelings. If Pisces can teach Aries the art of subtlety, this pairing is a keeper.

Pisces with Taurus:

Taurus is just the kind of partner that Pisces needs for the fairytale romance. Pisces will instantly make Taurus fall in love with them and that sweet way they have about them. Pisces is the big dreamer and creative of the zodiac, so role-playing and erotic games are what they will use to entice Taurus' libido. The Bull will respond to the sensual touches of the Fish, and you could say the rest is history. Both love luxury, so at least one should keep an eye on the purse strings to keep them from bankrupting themselves. They'll have enough to do in the bedroom to keep them busy anyway, so they won't be out blowing a lot of money. If they invest in silky sheets and all the fine accouterments to go along with them, they'll never want to leave!

Pisces with Gemini:

At first, Gemini will be all into Pisces' seductive ways and surreal approach to sex. Then, they'll realize that Pisces is for real, what you see is what you get; even with the love of donning costumes for bedroom romps, the Fish plays for keeps. Gemini will begin to get irritated with Pisces' sweetness, and pop off against them with a sharply witty tongue. Pisces will be crushed and think Gemini is a rude ass. Then it will be on a slow and steady decline from there. They should decide to call it a day before things get too ugly.

Pisces with Cancer:

While some matches are made in heaven, the one between these two water signs is made in the deep blue sea, where they both feel completely at home. They will spend so much time in the bedroom, they may get homesick for the waves, unless they're making their own on a waterbed. Pisces and Cancer will have to keep a stack of restaurant takeout menus on the nightstand or they may starve to death from all the energy they exert while mattress surfing. Outside the bedroom, if they ever come out, they will be able to have a solid foundation for their future together. Both love being homebodies, but will have a good time venturing out in the world, as long as they do it together. One of the best life partnerships of the zodiac!

Pisces with Leo:

Combine Water with Fire and you usually get steam, but not with this pair. Pisces may as well take a bucket of water and throw it on Leo because their fire will be doused completely. Pisces like romantic dinners in nice secluded corners with candlelight, flowers, and all the sweet whisperings about their fantasies. Leo wants all eyes on them, as they try to impress Pisces with boisterous tabletop dancing and public displays of affection. These differences can drive a permanent wedge between them, and even if in some weird instance they should make towards the bedroom, they really shouldn't go in, because they'll come out as enemies. Better to salvage some semblance of a friendship, if possible.

Pisces with Virgo:

Virgo will be attracted to Pisces' romantic ways and completely enraptured, at first. The first few times the couple gets between the sheets will be more than satisfying, with all the bells and whistles. Then Virgo will start to be critical of everything that Pisces does, which can seriously damage the Fish's sensitive side and cause them to withhold sex. That won't go over well for Virgo, who will retaliate, until they're playing tit for tat. If that weren't enough to take the bloom of the rose, Virgo works hard for material success, while Pisces works towards spiritual enlightenment. So they either need to quit before they begin, or know when to leave before it gets nasty, because doing the nasty is never going to be enough for these two.

Pisces with Libra:

These two can spend hours upon end in bed together making sweet love, because both signs are such romantics. They are also very creative when it comes to what they are going to do the next round. Pisces is highly imaginative and can always come up with something new for them to try. Libra is in to the Arts, so can "paint" a beautiful setting for their love nest. It's just too bad that issues manifest when it comes to planning a future together. Both love nice things and, as a result, are big spenders. The problems come when neither of the pair can hold onto the bucks. But, if they can work out money and debt issues, Pisces and Libra will be a lasting match.

Pisces with Scorpio:

This is another Water sign combo that is one for the books. Pisces wants someone with intensity that is on the same wavelength as them. Scorpio fits this requirement to a tee. Scorp will take control, which Pisces loves, and take them to unimaginable heights and back again. Pisces' adoration of the Scorpion will have them feeling like they won the trophy. Both are very intuitive and will know what the other is thinking and what they want without saying a word. They will take turns inventing new ways to keep it fresh for as long as they are still able to do it. This is one for "'til death do they part."

Pisces with Sagittarius:

Pisces and Sagittarius will break all the sexual rules when it comes to them getting together, so they may as well throw away all the manuals and create their own. Not a thing will be forbidden. Lusty Sag will have the passionate Fish swimming upstream, when they get going. But as soon as they leave the blissful bed, problems will pop up all over the place. Sagittarius' eye will start to wander and they'll look to faraway places for something strange to mix it up. This is an absolute no-no for Pisces, who will try yanking at Sag's leash, but it'll probably be too late. They'd be better off keeping each other as an emergency booty call than going for the long haul.

Pisces with Capricorn:

Pisces and Capricorn are on two separate planes when it comes to their intellectual abilities. Capricorn is a business genius and Pisces' intellect is connected to the universal mind. But sexually, they are so in sync they may as well be the same person. While the sex may not be earth shattering, it will be steady, and as comfortable as an old pair of slippers. Pisces brings all the sweetness to the relationship and Capricorn brings strength and stability to make this an everlasting pair.

Pisces with Aquarius:

Anyone looking at Pisces and Aquarius would think they'd be perfect for each other. With their broad-minded views on life and sex and even-tempered attitudes, these two would seem to be on the same page. The issue is that neither one wants to go through the trouble of starting the action, because they both need someone who takes charge. They're really good at talking about it, but that's where they end. They are much better as pals or BFF's since they'll probably never get around to doing the deed.

Pisces with Pisces:

Oh, the shame of it all! Pisces is so hot and into anything or everything that will turn on their partner. So two Pisces together should be fantastic, right? Nope. They are identical and bring out the absolute worse in each other. They're going to end up pouting or sulking, barely talking to each other. There'll be no need to withhold sex, because they won't be having any. Just forget about trying to be together and be good friends. There's nothing better than having a bestie that can read the other's mind!

Pisces Celebrities And Dirty, Sexy, Funny

Rihanna:

In *Cosmopolitan*[65], Rihanna talked about all the things she likes in the bedroom. She has always been very open about her sexuality and was very candid. She said that being submissive is fun in the bedroom, and that to her, she gets to be a lady in the act. To be able to have someone in charge and all macho is fun to her. She also said she likes being spanked and tied up. She wants it to be spontaneous, and would rather have her lover use his body, since you have to stop what you're doing and find the whip and chains, if you're going to go that route.

How Rihanna feels about sex is very typical of a Pisces. They love role-playing and it sounds like the Marque De Sade is exactly what she likes.

Ke$ha:

When Ke$ha was interviewed by Ryan Seacrest[66] for his radio show KIIS FM, she admitted that she's into having sex with supernatural beings. In fact, she claimed that she has had a couple of sexual encounters with one, but didn't know his name. She also said that she's really open to the whole idea.

Pisces is the most spiritual sign of the Zodiac and is said to easily move between the physical and the spiritual planes. So it would seem that spirits follow suit, and are hooking up with Ke$ha here on terra firma. But then again, there's always the possibility that she's crossing over to meet them in the spirit realm.

Olivia Wilde:

Olivia Wilde was very open about discussing her vajayjay on the *Glamour* sponsored monologue night, *These Girls*[67]. She said that after her divorce from her Italian prince husband, Tao Ruspoli, she felt as if her nether region had died. She went on to say that fiancé Jason Sudeikis has brought that dead area back to life in a big way. They now go at it like marathon runners from Kenya.

The Pisces woman likes a strong man who will take care of her. It sounds like Jason fits the bill by taking care of Olivia in a big way. Restoring life is nothing short of miraculous! Of course, Pisces believe in miracles more than any other sign and expect them to happen, so maybe Olivia just willed it into reality!

Eva Longoria:

In an interview for *Self*[68], Eva Longoria spoke candidly about the virtues of self-pleasuring with the Rabbit vibrator. She said that she was never very sexual until she started this practice, so it's a shame she hadn't come across it earlier. Eva went on to say that she buys Rabbits for all her girlfriends and that they squeal with delight upon opening. She also said that she likes for her man to be in charge, and that being submissive is very sexy. And silk scarves are a big plus!

Pisces love erotic games and if they don't have someone to play with, Eva proves they can play by themselves. They are also very compassionate and imaginative, so what better gift could she give her gal pals than the all-satisfying Rabbit!

Pisces Celebrity List

February 19:
Victoria Justice
Seal
Benicio Del Toro
Bellamy Young
Justine Bateman
Lee Marvin
Ray Winstone
Immortal Technique
Prince Andrew, Duke
   of York

February 20:
Rihanna
Sidney Poitier
Charles Barkley
Cindy Crawford
Nancy Wilson
Anthony Head
Kurt Cobain
Ansel Adams
French Stewart
Sandy Duncan
Ivana Trump
Lili Taylor
Chelsea Peretti
Gloria Vanderbilt

February 21:
Ashley Green
Rue Mcclanahan
Ellen Page
David Geffan
Alan Rickman
Kelsey Grammer
Chespirito
Jennifer Love Hewitt
Kelsey Grammer
Nina Simone
Wishbone
Charlotte Church
William Petersen
Tyne Daly
William Baldwin
Lidia Bastianich

February 22:
Mia Michaels
Drew Barrymore
Steve Irwin
Julius Erving
Robert Kardashian
Ted Kennedy
Thomas Jane
Sheldon Leonard
Kyle Maclachian

February 23:
Dakota Fanning
Peter Fonda
Emily Blunt
Skylar Grey
Aziz Ansari
Niecy Nash
Peter Fonda
Patricia Richardson
Johnny Winter

February 24:
Steve Jobs
Floyd Mayweather
Billy Zane
Kristin Davis
Emily Rudd
Abe Vigoda
Edward James Olmos
Sammy Kershaw
Emily Didonato
Barry Bostwick

February 25:
Sean Astin
George Hamilton
Rashida Jones
Justin Jeffre
Chelsea Handler
Carrot Top

Tea Leoni
Nancy Odell

February 26:
Erykah Badu
Michael Bolton
Fats Domino
Johnny Cash
Jackie Gleason
James Wan
Tony Randall
Ky-Mani Marley

February 27:
Jenni "JWoww" Farley
Elizabeth Taylor
Josh Groban
Rozonda "Chilli" Thomas
Chelsea Clinton
Kate Mara
John Steinbeck
Adam Baldwin
Timothy Spall
Joanne Woodward
James Worthy
Wendy Liebman
Donal Logue
Howard Hesseman
Johnny Van Zant

February 28:
Jason Aldean
Mario Andretti
Gilbert Gottfried
Bernadette Peters
Ali Larter
Mario Andretti
Rae Dawn Chong
John Turturro
Linus Pauling

February 29:
Ja Rule
Antonio Sabato Jr.
Dinah Shore
Tony Robbins
Tempest Storm
Dennis Farina

March 1:
Justine Bieber
Kesha Sebert
Booker T
Ron Howard
Lupita Nyongo
Mark-Paul Gosselaar
Ron Howard
Roger Daltrey
Alan Thicke
Catherine Bach
Javier Bardem

George Eads
Harry Belafonte
Tate Stevens
Maurice Benard
Chris Webber
Robert Conard
Lana Wood
Tim Daly

March 2:
Daniel Craig
Dr. Seuss
Jon Bon Jovi
Reggie Bush
Method Man
Desi Arnaz
Karen Carpenter
Bryce Dallas Howard
Laraine Newman

March 3:
Buddy Valastro
Herschel Walker
Jessica Biel
Jackie Joyner-Kersee
Julie Bowen
Herschel Walker
James Doohan
Tyler Florence
Miranda Richardson
Aarti Mann

March 4:
Bobbi Kristina Brown
Patricia Heaton
Erin Heatherton
Patsy Kensit
Kevin Johnson
Chaz Bono
Catherine O'Hara

March 5:
Eva Mendes
Joel Osteen
Andy Gibb
Penn Jillette
Niki Taylor
Teena Marie
Kimberly Mccullough
Talia Balsom
Rex Harrison
Dean Stockwell
Elaine Paige

March 6:
Shaquille O'Neal
Tom Arnold
Mary Wilson
Connie Britton
Tom Arnold
Moira Kelly
Rob Reiner
DL Hughley

Stedman Graham
Jacklyn Zeman

March 7:
Bryan Cranston
Ivan Lendl
Laura Prepon
Rachel Weisz
TJ Thyme
Wanda Sykes
John Heard
Taylor Dayne
Willard Scott
Peter Sarsgaard
Michael Eisner

March 8:
Kat Von D
Hines Ward
Freddie Prinze Jr.
Micky Dolenz
James Van Der Beek
Camryn Manheim
Aidan Quinn
Lester Holt
Lynn Redgrave
Cyd Charisse

March 9:
Bow Wow
Matthew Gray Gubler

Emmanuel Lewis
Brittany Snow
Bobby Fischer
Keely Smith
Raul Julia
Juliette Binoche
Mary Murphy
Mickey Gilley
Robin Trower

March 10:
Carrie Underwood
Chuck Norris
Sharon Stone
Robin Thicke
Olivia Wilde
Jasmine Guy
Paget Brewster
John Hamm
Prince Edward, Earl of
    Wessex
Barbara Corcoran
Shannon Tweet

March 11:
Johnny Knoxville
Thora Birch
Terrenc Howard
Alex Kingston
Rupert Murdoch
Joel Madden

Benji Madden
Shemp Howard
Bobby McFerrin
Simon Curtis
Fugative

March 12:
James Taylor
Liza Minelli
Marlon Jackson
Darrly Strawberry
Aaron Eckhart
Courtney B. Vance
Barbara Feldon
Gordn MacRae
Jack Kerouac
Al Jarreau

March 13:
Common
Dana Delany
Peaches Geldof
Noel Fisher
William H. Macy
Ernie Hirsch
Annabeth Gish
Neil Sedaka
Rachael Bella

March 14:
Sasha Grey
Billy Crystal
Aamir Khan
Taylor Hanson
Michael Caine
Quincy Jones
Grace Park
Jamie Bell
Este Haim
Megan Follows
Tamara Tunie
Chris Klein
Penny Johnson

March 15:
Eva Longoria
Sly Stone
Will I Am
Bret Michaels
Fabio
Young Buck
Kim Raver
Judd Hirsch

March 16:
Flavor Flav
Erik Estrada
Lauren Graham
William Garber
Jerry Lewis

Tim Hardaway Jr.
Danny Brown
Rupert Sanders
Tim Kang
Bernardo Bertolucci
Sophie Hunter

March 17:
Hozier
Kurt Russell
Rob Kardashian
Gary Sinise
Tamar Braxton
Rob Lowe
Mia Hamm
Nat King Cole
Coco Austin
Alexander McQueen
Nicky Jam
Patrick Duffy

March 18:
Adam Levine
Vanessa Williams
Lily Collins
Bonnie Blair
Dane Cook
Queen Latifah
Irene Cara
Wilson Pickett
Mike Rowe

Charley Pride
Peter Graves
Sophia Myles

March 19:
Jake Webber
Glenn Close
Ursula Andress
Bruce Willis
Moms Mabley

March 20:
Ozzie Nelson
Hal Linden
Fred Rogers
Spike Lee
Bobby Orr
Holly Hunter
Carl Reiner
Vera Lynn
Jerry Reed
Kathy Ireland
William Hurt
Pat Riley

About Sabra Ricci

Courtesy of Justine Belson

Sabra Ricci is a professional astrologer and private chef with a clientele that includes some of the biggest names in Hollywood. Ricci has appeared on many national television shows, including *Chelsea Lately* and the *Today Show,* and is a frequent guest on a variety of radio shows, most recently with a monthly Astrology segment on Jenny McCarthy's SiriusXM Radio Show, *Dirty, Sexy, Funny.* She has been featured in several publications, such as *Life &*

Style, OK!, Woman's Day, The Daily Mail UK, and *Self* magazines. She also contributes regularly to *About.com*, the New York Times-based website, *Tarot.com, DailyHoroscope.com,* and *GabbyandLaird.com*, Gabrielle Reece and Laird Hamilton's fitness and lifestyle website. Her daily astrology forecast can be found on the *Chicago Sun-Times: Splash* website. She is the author of *Lobster for Leos, Cookies for Capricorns: An Astrology Lover's Cookbook* and *Sexy Star Sign Cooking: An Astrology Cookbook for Lovers*, which combines her love of Astrology and passion for cooking. Ricci lives in Santa Monica, California with her husband, Ferenc.

www.sabraricci.com

www.sabraricciastrology.com

www.facebook.com/pages/Sabra-Ricci/

@Mauichef

instagram.com/Mauichefsabra

About Jenny McCarthy

Courtesy of Anthony Tahlier

Jenny McCarthy is the author of ten books, including the *New York Times* bestsellers *Belly Laughs: The Naked Truth About Pregnancy and Childbirth*; *Baby Laughs: The Naked Truth About the First Year of Mommyhood*; *Louder Than Words: A Mother's Journey in Healing Autism*; *Love, Lust & Faking It: The Naked Truth About Sex, Lies, and True Romance*; and *Bad Habits: The Confessions of a Recovering Catholic*. Getting her start as the host of MTV's hugely popular dating show *Singled Out*, McCarthy has had a high-profile television and film career and has been a guest on virtually every television talk show, from *The Oprah Winfrey Show*, *Larry King Live*, *The View*, *The Ellen DeGeneres Show*, and *Late Night with David Letterman*, to *Conan*, *Hannity & Colmes*, and *The Howard Stern Show*. A former co-host of ABC's *The View*, she also co-hosts *Dick Clark's New Year's Rockin' Eve* with Ryan Seacrest, writes an advice column for the *Chicago Sun-Times*, tours nationally for her *Dirty, Sexy, Funny* stand up-show, hosts SiriusXM Radio's *Dirty, Sexy, Funny with Jenny McCarthy*, and co-stars in A&E's *Donnie Loves Jenny*. She lives in Weehawken, New Jersey with son, Evan and husband, Donnie.

www.jennymccarthy.com

facebook.com/jennymccarthyofficial

@jennymccarthy

instagram.com/jennymccarthy

End Notes

1 Howard Stern Interview YOU TUBE Uploaded on May 10, 2011, (https://www.youtube.com/watch?v=cy8PMvhQvrg)

2 Reagan Alexander 10/03/2014 at 2:45 PM EDT PEOPLE (http://www.people.com/article/robert-downey-jr-marriage-secrets-judge-premiere)

3 Andrew Goldman, Jan 7, 2009 @ 11:00AM ELLE (http://www.elle.com/culture/celebrities/a9605/livin-on-the-edge-284253/)

4 David Marchese SPIN (http://www.spin.com/articles/8-wild-revelations-steven-tylers-memoir/)

5 Rachel Maresca / New York Daily News / Wednesday, November 12, 2013, 12:17 PM NY DAILY NEWS (http://www.nydailynews.com/entertainment/gossip/lady-gaga-open-threesome-boyfriend-taylor-kinney-article-1.1515413)

6 NicoleI Eggenberger Celebrity News Nov 12 2013 AT 6:20PM US WEEKLY (http://www.usmagazine.com/celebrity-news/news/lady-gaga-is-in-a-monogamous-relationship-with-boyfriend-taylor-kinney-but-open-to-a-threesome-20131211)

7 Christa D'Souza 04 September 2012 VOGUE (http://www.vogue.co.uk/news/2012/09/04/kristen-stewart-vogue-cover-interview)

[8] Natalie Finn Tue., June 3, 2008 5:25 PM PDT EONLINE (http://www.eonline.com/news/1603/megan-a-fox-in-heat)

[9] Peter Sheridan For THE MAIL ON SUNDAY Published: 17:01 EST, 14 February 2015 | Updated: 07:08 EST, 15 February 2015

[10] Moviefone Staff Posted November 9th, 2011 MOVIEFOE (http://news.moviefone.com/2011/11/09/george-clooney-rolling-stone/)

[11] VIBE / October 6, 2013 http://www.vibe.com/2013/10/chris-brown-says-he-lost-his-virginity-age-8/

[12] Suzannah Ramsdale 11:10 | 01 May 2012 MARIE CLAIRE (http://www.marieclaire.co.uk/news/celebrity/536025/gwyneth-paltrow-and-zoe-saldane-talk-favourite-sex-positions.html#index=1)

[13] Chelsea White Published: 15:39 EST, 8 May 2014 | Updated: 21:21 EST, 8 May 2014 DAILY MAIL (http://www.dailymail.co.uk/tvshowbiz/article-2623721/Planes-trains-automobiles-Zoe-Saldana-reveals-naughtiest-places-shes-sex.html)

[14] Chiderah Monde / NEW YORK DAILY NEWS / Sunday, August 4, 2013, 1:02 PM

[15] Sarv Kreindler December 4, 2014 9:03 AM ET BRAVO (http://www.bravotv.com/the-daily-dish/watch-lisa-vanderpump-grill-andy-cohen)

[16] Laura Schreffler Updated: 12:30 EST, 23 November 2011 DAILY MAIL UK (http://www.dailymail.co.uk/tvshowbiz/article-2064933/Angelina-Jolie-Im-bad-girl-belongs-Brad-Pitt.html)

[17] Stephen M. Silverman 07/09/2003 at 11:00 AM EDT PEOPLE (http://www.people.com/people/article/0,,626414,00.html)

[18] Scott Huver LA CONFIDENTIAL MAGAZINE (http://la-confidential-magazine.com/personalities/articles/masters-of-sex-star-lizzy-caplan-on-playing-virginia-johnson-funny-sex-scenes)

[19] Written By: Russell V Nov 20, 2014 | 4:30 AM VLADTV (http://www.vladtv.com/blog/178893/kevin-harts-ex-talks-about-sex-skills-says-hart-put-it-down/)

[20] Annabel Brog Posted 29 Wed October ELLE UK (http://www.elleuk.com/now-trending/benedict-cumberbatch-talks-sherlock-and-sex)

[21] Nicole Eggenberger Entertainment Jan 8, 2014 at 4:30PM US MAGAZINE (http://www.usmagazine.com/entertainment/news/margot-robbie-talks-wolf-of-wall-street-sex-scenes-auditioning-with-leonardo-dicaprio-201481)

[22] Antoinette Bueno March 13, 2012 12:08 PM (https://celebrity.yahoo.com/news/jessica-simpson-her-unstoppable-sex-drive-160800212.html)

[23] Nardine Saad December 19, 2013, 11:31AM LA TIMES (http://www.latimes.com/entertainment/gossip/la-et-mg-jennifer-lawrence-sex-toy-maid-conan-wetting-bed-20131219-story.html)

[24] The X-rated Interview – page 5 THE ADVOCATE (http://www.ultramadonna.com/en/articles/18/the_xrated_interview/view/5)

[25] theruffwriter Fri, January 23, 2015 6:07pm EDT http://hollywoodlife.com/2015/01/23/jennifer-lopez-disses-ex-boyfriends-looks-exes-watch-what-happens-live/

[26] THE HUFFINGTON POST UK Posted: 08/08/2011 10:56BST | Updated: 08/10/2011 10:12 BST (http://www.huffingtonpost.co.uk/2011/08/08/antonio-banderas-interview-madonna-penelope-pedro_n_920772.html)

[27] Wednesday, Nov 1, 2000 10:44 AM PDT (http://www.salon.com/2000/11/01/npwed_20/)

[28] Zach Johnson Celebrity News July 17, 2013 at 3:20PM US WEEKLY (http://www.usmagazine.com/celebrity-news/news/jason-sudeikis-credits-sex-with-olivia-wilde-for-his-weight-loss-201317)

[29] HUFF POST ENTERTAINMENT Posted 09/27/2010 11:32 am EDT | Updated: 05/25/2011 1:35 pm EDT (http://www.huffingtonpost.com/2009/07/15/jada-pinkett-smith-adds-l_n_233493.html)

[30] K Maine YOURTANGO.COM (http://www.yourtango.com/201172258/emmy-rossum-and-chelsea-handler-talk-realistic-camera-sex)

[31] Hollywoodlifeintern Wed, September 3, 2014 3:52pm EDT Cosmopolitan 2014 HOLLYWOODLIFE (http://hollywoodlife.com/2014/09/03/emmy-rossum-one-night-stand-easy-cosmopolitan-interview-fiona/)

[32] David Resin April 15, 2011 PLAYBOY (http://www.playboy.com/articles/charlie-sheen-interview)

[33] Leanne Bayley | Thursday, 15 January 2015 GLAMOUR News (http://www.glamourmagazine.co.uk/news/celebrity/2015/01/15/gwyneth-paltrow-howard-stern-radio-show-quotes-2015)

[34] Chiderah Monde / NEW YORK DAILY NEWS / Tuesday, March 19, 2013, 12:29 PM April GQ, (http://www.nydailynews.com/entertainment/gossip/bruno-mars-sex-great-party-starter-article-1.1292779)

[35] USWeekly Staff, Celebrity News Feb. 10, 2010 at 8:45AM USWEEKLY (http://www.usmagazine.com/celebrity-news/news/john-mayer-jessica-simpson-was-crazy-2010102)

[36] Lily Harrison Tue., Feb. 10, 2015 4:15 PM PST EONLINE (http://www.eonline.com/news/624313/kim-kardashian-pees-on-her-spanx-reveals-her-favorite-sex-position-more-cringe-worthy-confessions)

[37] NADINE DENINNO Wed, Feb 11, 2015 | 11:33 AM OK!, Cara Delevingne, LOVE MAGAZINE September 2015

http://okmagazine.com/photos/kim-kardashian-love-magazine-inter-view-naked-photos-quotes/photo/1001209246/

38 GLAMOUR January 30, 2015 (http://www.glamour.com/enter-tainment/blogs/obsessed/2015/01/glamour-50-shades-of-grey-cover)

39 Zach Johnson Wed., Jun. 4, 2014 8:01 AM PDT EONLINE (http://www.eonline.com/news/548031/katy-perry-talks-exes-russell-brand-and-john-mayer-reveals-the-longest-she-s-gone-without-sex)

40 Jackalz on June6, 2012 ENTERTAINMENT NEWS Celeb Dirty Laundry (http://www.celebdirtylaundry.com/2012/katy-perry-craves-sex-with-rihanna-0606/)

41 Daily Mail Reporter Published: 21:00 EST, 20 February 2014 | Updated: 09:02 EST, 21 February 2014 DAILY MAIL.COM, Gayle King, CBS This Morning (http://www.dailymail.co.uk/tvshowbiz/article-2564452/Leonardo-DiCaprio-reveals-looks-woman-NOT-supermodel-beauty.html)

42 Sandra Clark Mon, March 11, 2013 9:27pm EDT HOLLYWOOD LIFE The Howard Stern Show (http://hollywoodlife.com/2013/03/11/brandi-glanville-gerard-but-ler-sex-howard-stern-show/)

43 Jessica Grose July 25 2011 10:28 AM SLATE (http://www.slate.com/articles/arts/culturebox/2011/07/questions_for_ryan_gosling.html)

44 HUFF POST ENTERTAINMENT Posted: 01/10/2011 10:07 am EST | Updated: 05/25/2011 6:25 pm EDT (http://www.huffington-post.com/2011/01/10/ryan-gosling-sex-scene-wi_n_806678.html)

45 Martha Sorren 05.30.2014 Entertainment BUSTLE (http://www.bustle.com/articles/26354-angelina-jolie-wears-her-maleficent-horns-in-bed-5-other-brangelina-sex-facts)

46 Bang Showbiz | Lifestyle / Showbiz | 15 December 2014 contact-music.com (http://hub.contactmusic.com/scarlett-johansson/news/scarlett-johansson-sex-scenes-are-liberat-ing_4508488)

[47] DAILY MAIL.COM Last updated at 17:42 10 October 2006 (http://www.dailymail.co.uk/tvshowbiz/article-409657/Scarlett-Johansson-takes-HIV-tests-year-says-shes-promiscuous.html)

[48] timfxplant Sun, December 14, 2014 9:17pm EDT HOLLY-WOOD LIFE http://hollywoodlife.com/2014/12/14/scarlett-johansson-sex-scenes-most-fascinating-people-2014-interview/

[49] Josh Kurp 02.10.15 UPROXX http://uproxx.com/webculture/2015/02/chrissy-teigen-made-john-legend-squirm-when-she-revealed-the-best-place-theyve-had-public-sex/

[50] Laurie Sandell Apr 28, 2014 @ 8:55AM COSMOLOLITAN (http://www.cosmopolitan.com/entertainment/news/a24251/chrissy-teigen-on-june-2014-cosmo/)

[51] COSMOPOLITAN 9:45AM, Mar 17, 2014 (http://www.cosmopolitan.com.au/celebrity/celebrity-gossip/2014/3/miley-cyrus-offers-up-sex-tips-on-twitter/)

[52] Eliana Dockterman | May 1, 2014 ELLE (http://time.com/84432/5-things-we-learned-from-mileys-elle-interview/)

[53] HUFFPOST CELEBRITY Posted 05/21/2012 2:02 pm EDT | Updated: 05/21/2012 2:02 pm EDT http://www.huffingtonpost.com/2012/05/21/miley-cyrus-sex-beautiful-magical-thing_n_1533181.html

[54] Tom Sykes 10.09.14 THE DAILY BEAST, (http://www.thedailybeast.com/articles/2014/10/09/sex-drugs-and-kate-moss-secrets-of-a-wild-supermodel.html)

[55] Melissa Thompson 00:00, 17 May 2013 MIRROR (http://www.mirror.co.uk/3am/celebrity-news/bradley-cooper-i-love-company-1893833)

[56] HUFF POST Posted 10/05/2010 2:45pm EDT | Updated: 05/25/2011 5:55 pm EDT

(http://www.huffingtonpost.com/2010/10/05/betty-white-talks-sex-agi_n_751306.html)

[57] Stuart Jeffries, Sunday 3 March 2013 14:00 EST THE GUARDIAN US (http://www.theguardian.com/culture/2013/mar/03/jude-law-phone-hacking-40-side-effects)

[58] Monday, February 06, 2006, THE CORSAIR (http://ronmwangaguhunga.blogspot.com/2006/02/daisy-wright-jude-laws-not-small-at.html)

[59] Gillian Flynn September 9, 2014 GLAMOUR OCTOBER ISSUE (http://www.glamour.com/entertainment/blogs/obsessed/2014/09/ros amund-pike-gillian-flynn-gone-girl-interview)

[60] Andrew Goldman Jan 20, 2010 @ 10:00 AM (http://www.elle.com/culture/movies-tv/a10832/wise-guy-bill-maher-392832/)

[61] Chris Spargo April 10, 2013 LOGO NEW NOW NEXT, Jay Leno THE TONIGHT SHOW (http://www.newnownext.com/rebel-wilson-talks-first-sex-scene-nunchucks-watch/04/2013/)

[62] Karishma Sarkari for DAILY MAIL AUSTRALIA Published: 23:09 EST, 29 November 2014 | Updated: 11:23 EST, 30 November 2014 (http://www.dailymail.co.uk/tvshowbiz/article-2854620/Cirque-du-Fat-Amy-Comedian-Rebel-Wilson-talks-training-famed-acrobats-opening-sequence-Pitch-Perfect-2.html)

[63] Todd Gilchrist January 20, 20ll pro.boxoffice.com (http://pro.boxoffice.com/news/2011-01-interview-how-ashton-kutcher-and-natalie-portman-connected-in-no-strings-attached)

[64] K.C. Blumm 02/13/2015 at 03:00 PM EST PEOPLE (http://www.people.com/article/ashton-kutcher-sex-mila-kunis-best-advice-taylor-swift)

[65] Zoe Ruderman MAR 31, 2011 @ 12:31 PM Cosmopolitan (http://www.cosmopolitan.com/entertainment/celebs/news/a9167/rih anna-rolling-stone-interview-being-submissive/)

66 Ray Rahman Posted September 27 2012 – 2:47 PM EDT ENTER-
TAINMENT WEEKLY, Ryan Seacrest on KIIS FM
(http://www.ew.com/article/2012/09/27/kesha-sex-with-ghost)

67 USWeekly Staff Celebrity News Oct. 9, 2012 at 6:30PM US
WEEKLY These Girls GLAMOUR
(http://www.usmagazine.com/celebrity-news/news/olivia-wilde-
jason-sudeikis-and-i-have-sex-like-kenyan-marathon-runners-
2012910)

68 Amy McCarthy 02.18.2014 Lifestyle BUSTLE, SELF MAGAZINE
(http://www.bustle.com/articles/15846-15-celebrities-who-love-their-
sex-toys-barbara-walters-jennifer-lawrence-more/page/1)

Printed in Great Britain
by Amazon